A.G. RIZZOLI

Architect of Magnificent Visions

A.G. RIZZOLI

OF MAGI

ARCHITECT
NIFICENT
VISIONS

by Jo Farb Hernandez, John Beardsley,
and Roger Cardinal

Harry N. Abrams, Inc., Publishers,
in association with the
San Diego Museum of Art

Published on the occasion of "A. G. Rizzoli:
Architect of Magnificent Visions," an exhibition
organized and circulated by the San Diego
Museum of Art

EXHIBITION SCHEDULE:
San Diego Museum of Art
March 22–May 18, 1997

High Museum of Art
September 6–November 29, 1997

Museum of American Folk Art
January 10–March 8, 1998

San Francisco Museum of Modern Art
March 28–May 24, 1998

EDITOR: Ruth A. Peltason
DESIGNER: Judith Hudson

CAPTIONS
Page 1: *Mother Symbolically Recaptured/*
The Kathredal (detail). 1937
Page 4: *Mr. O. A. Deichmann's Mother*
Symbolically Sketched/Toure D'Longevity
(detail). 1938

LIBRARY OF CONGRESS
CATALOGING–IN–PUBLICATION DATA
Hernandez, Jo Farb.
A. G. Rizzoli : architect of magnificent visions /
by Jo Farb Hernandez, John Beardsley, and
Roger Cardinal.
    p.   cm.
Includes bibliographical references.
ISBN 0–8109–4293–3. — ISBN 0–937108–20–0 (pbk.)
1. Rizzoli, Achilles G., 1896–1981.
2. Architects—United States—Biography.
3. Eclecticism in architecture—United States.
I. Rizzoli, Achilles G., 1896–1981. II. Beardsley,
John. III. Cardinal, Roger. IV. San Diego Museum
of Art. V. Title.
NA737.R547H47 1997
720'.92—dc20
[B]   96–42329

Published in 1997 by Harry N. Abrams,
Incorporated, New York
A Times Mirror Company

Printed and bound in Japan

PHOTOGRAPH CREDITS
All photographs are by Ben Blackwell except
for the following: Wendy Idele, pages 40, 42–43,
92, 114; The Ames Gallery, pages 14–15, 17, 19
(bottom), 36 (bottom right), 67, 73–76, 86 (bottom)

CONTENTS

Contrary to Hollywood myth, artists are not usually "discovered" in dramatic encounters, heroically rescued from obscurity and posthumously heralded by the critical establishment.

Of course, there are exceptions.

The story of the discovery of the work of Achilles Rizzoli, its subsequent rescue by a passionate collector, and the recognition of the artist and his work by the scholarly community is both exciting and heartening. It is a story of passion and isolation, compelling persistence and dedication, and luck. And now, at the culmination of concerted effort, the work is receiving the attention it so richly deserves.

For me, the story began with a degree of reluctance and not a small amount of skepticism. Impassioned pleas and urgent correspondence regarding "important new finds" and invitations to view "must see" collections are not unusual in the course of my work.

Museum professionals might be forgiven for becoming somewhat jaded after many disappointments and aesthetic dead ends. But from time to time, with just enough tantalizing regularity to keep hope alive, one may encounter the truly remarkable, the genuine "find."

This time, Bonnie Grossman issued the invitation, and the promise of viewing a remarkable group of works, and the possibility of sharing Bonnie's reliable enthusiasm, led me to Berkeley. There, in a loft, was the accumulated life's work of someone named Achilles Rizzoli, which had been lovingly stored and catalogued.

The sheer scope of the collection presented to me was daunting – hundreds of sheets of drawings and schematic sketches were piled in formidable stacks. There were mountains of books and letters, reams of notes, countless renderings – a graphic encyclopedia of a secret and reclusive artistic exigency.

The work was stunning: meticulous, compulsive, expansive, and beguiling. Rendered in the sure hand of an erudite visionary, it had the fastidious air of the technically adroit and the wondrous sense of the innocent prodigy. By the time we had scrutinized the material and discussed the intimidating range of the oeuvre, I was convinced that the work deserved to be seen by a wider audience.

The natural choice to curate the project was Jo Farb Hernandez, a commanding presence in the emerging universe of artists who reside on the outskirts of traditional training and are often eschewed by the traditional art establishment. And with the enthusiastic encouragement of Harry N. Abrams, Inc., and the commitment of contributors John Beardsley and Roger Cardinal, the project moved forward.

The Trustees of the San Diego Museum of Art were early supporters of this effort. They seemed to sense, as did I, that there was something special afoot here – something richly infused with a kind of reluctant genius, something worth studying and offering to the community at large.

Everyone who came in contact with the work became an enthusiast, from the museum's head of publications, David Hewitt, whose contribution to this publication was invaluable, to the registrar, Louis Goldich, who collected and oversaw the preparation and transport of the works. Among the other members of the museum's staff who contributed to making the exhibition a success were Holly Witchey, associate curator, European art/prints and drawings; Mitchell Gaul, head of design and installation; Mardi Snow, public relations manager; David Kencik, administrative assistant collections and rights and reproductions; Claire Cecil, special exhibitions assistant; and Cheryl Baker, secretary. I would also like to extend my thanks to Ruth Peltason and her staff at Harry N. Abrams, Inc. Further deserving of recognition are Susan Else and Sam Hernandez.

But it is to Bonnie Grossman that the credit must go for rescuing and preserving this remarkable work, and for recognizing its value. Hers is the kind of compassionate commitment so rarely seen in the art world; she cares deeply for this nearly neglected and potentially forgotten artist. Without her vision, there would be no exhibition, no book, or finally, no gathering of his work.

This presentation helps to restore one's faith in the spirit of art; it reveals the sometimes shrouded genius that dwells oft-neglected in our midst, and ultimately, it demonstrates the value of heroic dedication to investigation of the fringes of acceptance, in which so much worthy expression exists.

Steven L. Brezzo
Director, San Diego Museum of Art

AMPLIFYING
ACHILLES

BY BONNIE GROSSMAN

Amazing . . . fantastic . . . incredible! What words do I use to describe the new world that I had entered? Like Alice, I had fallen down the rabbit hole and found myself in an enchanted realm, a world of multifaceted words and images unlike anything I had ever seen or imagined . . . a Wonderland beyond belief.

The White Rabbit appeared to me in the form of a young woman. On July 12, 1990, she arrived at my gallery with a small collection of drawings she wanted to sell. The moment I saw them I was electrified. These were the creations of a wildly original mind. There were four architectural drawings and what looked like an illuminated list. All were precisely rendered, yet their meanings were obscure. They seemed to hint at something that the artist knew – but did not disclose. No history was offered with the pictures; as for the artist, he was unknown. The woman had found the work some twelve or fifteen years earlier in a house whose recent occupant had fallen ill or died. Four of the pieces were in color. One was glued to redwood board; one had been folded in half; the remaining two, though framed, were backed with corrosive chipboard. The larger of these was unglassed, protected only by crumbling cellophane. The brilliance of these pieces far outweighed their questionable condition. All were signed, or rather "delineated," by a variety of people with unusual names – Grandicosti, Copenhagen, and Angelhart. In addition, there were thirty-nine sheets of vellum. Each of these measured two by three feet and was a dense web of prose, poetry, and architectural renderings. All were done in pencil, and all signed A. G. Rizzoli.

What to do with this mesmerizing assortment? I pored over each line, each word, wanting to learn more about the work and its creator. The penciled pieces provided real names, unlike the fanciful color pieces. Impatiently, I followed up each clue and soon located the artist's great-nephew. Surprised by my phone call, he told me he had lots of his uncle's "stuff" in his garage. We arranged a meeting.

The garage door was open. It was hard to know where to look first. The largest drawings were piled on the rafters. They were still glued to redwood boards, just as Rizzoli had left them decades ago. Some were water-damaged, one had been chewed by mice, another was speckled with insect holes. A few flimsily framed pieces were tacked to the walls of the garage. Hundreds of the vellums were rolled up and secured with rubber bands. Other notes and papers were loosely piled in boxes. My heart was pounding – I had uncovered a great treasure.

The nephew could tell me almost nothing about his great-uncle. He did refer to him as Uncle Achilles, so at least I now knew what the "A" of "A. G." stood for. He suggested that I talk to his mother, Rizzoli's only niece. From her, I learned that the family had lived in Marin County. At the Marin County Hall of Records I turned up only one official document – a death certificate for Innocente Rizzoli, A. G.'s father. But that single piece of paper yielded important information: the name of the place where Innocente was born and the astonishing revelation that he had committed suicide in 1915, but that his remains were only discovered twenty-one years later. Since the day I found that piece of paper, each further discovery has made the Rizzoli story "curioser and curioser."

To what can I compare my adventure? The unraveling of the life of A. G. Rizzoli might be likened to peeling back the thin layers of an onion. Behind each layer I found another layer, another tantalizing clue. The clues led me around the world, to cousins of the Rizzoli family in Centovalli, near the Swiss-Italian border, and to some twenty people in California who knew A. G. and who, through phone conversations and personal interviews, provided observations and experiences that I could develop into a personal history. Thus, I had the rare opportunity to re-create a life story, using these interviews, the papers that Rizzoli left behind, and his art. What my research revealed was a witty, well-read, imaginative, intelligent, and caring loner. Because of this quest I often feel that I "know" A. G. . . . that A. G. and I have come to "know" each other.

Rizzoli loved to construct and reconstruct words – anagrams, acronyms, and neologisms. After years of poring over his seductive writing, I still find myself looking for a concealed meaning in the first letters of a title or trying to unscramble hidden puns and anagrams. My adventure in Wonderland will probably never end. Rizzoli has given me a new way to see everything, and the more I look, the more I think I see. Now I realize that there is always something hidden below the surface, always one more layer. . . .

ACKNOWLEDGMENTS

N. L. was the illusive White Rabbit who enticed me to set out on this merry chase, an absorbing quest that first led me to Gary Grauberger. In response to his wife, Marina's, very wise counsel, the Grauberger family had preserved the vast bulk of their great-uncle's work. Gary's mother, Evelyn Codoni Grauberger, was responsible for her uncle in his final years, and she and her family graciously shared with me what little they knew of their family history. The ensuing research, in turn, provided them with the framework of their unimagined background.

When I fell down the rabbit hole, I pulled a fair number of people in along with me. There to witness the magic moment I first laid eyes on a Rizzoli was my devoted and wonderful assistant, Anne Civitano. She has worked diligently to keep abreast of and organize the vast body of material that has been uncovered. John MacGregor not only validated my opinion about this discovery, but joined me for much of the initial research and wrote the first published article introducing this event which he described as ". . . rare even in the extraordinary annals of Outsider Art." John MacGregor's articles and his many lectures were significant in introducing Rizzoli to the world. In particular, I owe John a special debt for the introduction to Roger Cardinal and his wife, Agnes.

So many people responded to queries with gracious offers of assistance. Lauren Cheda and Rae Codoni, both from old Marin County families, helped with some of the most basic Rizzoli history. Gerry Holt maintained a lifelong connection with A. G. that dates back to 1939, when they were coworkers at the architectural office of Otto A. Deichmann. Margaret Griffin, Violetta Autumn, and Wayne Osaki also shared their recollections of the Deichmann office and the artist. Shirley Bersie Lobanoff; her cousin, Virginia Entwistle Bagatelos; Beverly Guardino; Grace Popich Hall, her sisters and brother; Katherine O'Grady Healy; I. P. Sicotte, Jr.; the D'India, Capobianco, and Foley families, all friends and neighbors – reached into their past to recall what they could of the man who immortalized many of them in his drawings. To the many named and unnamed individuals who answered my unusual, sometimes personal, often probing questions with grace, my sincere gratitude.

My steadfast husband, Sy, who has never flagged in his support of the project, braved far too much salami and Chianti when he guided me along the Alpen roads in my attempt to reconstruct the Rizzoli family tree. Filomena Giossi Guidi was key in our locating Clelia Fiscalini Rizzoli and her son, Fernando. Our friend Vittoria Ceretti made and translated all our telephone calls from Milan, and searched out and sent to us any material from the Italian press that she thought pertinent to our quest. Bianca Guareschi, Luigi De Moliner, and Federico Buffa were indispensable to our research in and around Milan.

Waverly Lowell, Gray Brechin, and Don Andrieni helped with discoveries in the area of architecture, and Kevin Day, a student at U. C. Berkeley, fell so completely under the spell that he wrote his masters thesis on Rizzoli, thereby making us the recipient of his insights and fresh perspective. Tony Civitano facilitated and consulted in identifying the appropriate copying machines needed to make the many thousands of copies that were required for all this research.

For an incredibly sensitive job of restoration, I relied solely on Erik Martin and Brian Hourican of Something Special. They made the thoughtful decisions necessary to manage the enormously time-consuming treatment, conservation, and framing of the entire collection. Over the years they have continued to maintain the collection, reframing the work under sometimes impossible deadlines as needs changed.

So many people supported my initial efforts to exhibit Rizzoli's work and validated my high regard for it. I would especially like to acknowledge Wanda Corn, Lynda Roscoe Hartigan, and Phil Linhares for their continued support and belief in the project. Throughout I have received good counsel from them, as well as from Joe Corn, Eugene Metcalf, and Joanne Cubbs.

Pat Ferrero's enthusiasm for the documentary film project has been inspirational. The team of consultants that she has put together continues to add dimension and insight to the project. The devotion that Pat and scriptwriter Sharon Wood brought, along with their willingness to share information, have helped to round out our perspective on A. G. R.

Thanks also to Bill Grose and Claire Carlevaro, both of whom have been generous and supportive; to Irwin Mayers for the many book searches; to Ann Bernauer and Helen Bersie for important initial research; to Susan Brandabur, Margaret Moulton, and Rob Schaeffer. Thanks to the writers – Eve Kahn, Jaime Wolfe, Marcia McKean, and Linda Monko – who have previously translated the power of Rizzoli's work into words; and to Irene Elmer. And to Everett Dulit and Rachel Goodman Edelson, who graciously offered their professional perspectives, special thanks.

Not surprisingly, over the years others have found themselves ensnared by the magic of Rizzoli and have offered generous support and counsel. Jo Farb Hernandez has had interest from the moment she laid eyes on the work in the first days it was spread around the gallery. She has been both tenacious and supportive, and I'm sure A. G. will have designed a wonderful heavenly home for her. Steve Brezzo flew up to Berkeley in the summer of 1992 to see the work and begin negotiations on behalf of the San Diego Museum of Art. His interest has never faltered. Ruth Peltason of Harry N. Abrams, Inc., has been constant in her eagerness to publish this material. I owe her a great debt for the professionalism with which she has handled the publication and people associated with it. Roger Cardinal has been a great joy to know as a friend, and of course, his scholarship on Rizzoli enriches us all. John Beardsley, the newest recruit to Wonderland, is a most welcome addition. His insights and contribution have provided a new energy and enthusiasm.

It is regrettable but inevitable that so many of the principals in this project have fallen ill or died before the dream was realized. But I often feel that A. G. Rizzoli, my own Cheshire Cat, sits on my shoulder grinning, and whispering in my ear, "Yes, yes, this is what I want!"

"DIVINE
DESIGN
THE LIFE AND WORKS OF A.G. RIZZOLI
DELIGHTS"

BY JO FARB HERNANDEZ

Visualize a perfect world.

You, the esteemed founder (superior in every way to your everyday self), would proclaim the essential goodness of your inspired creation, and be lauded for your utopian vision. Full of peace and beauty, your world would be protected by heroes who had conquered the forces of evil. The buildings gracing its cities would be grand and spacious, majestic yet inviting. It would be a world of people in different professions working together to foster the common good. It would be a time of spirituality, justice, and morality – a time of heaven on earth.

For most of us, dreaming of a world more to our liking is a pleasant momentary diversion, a fantasy soon abandoned. For others, however, the vision of an alternate world becomes more and more absorbing, demanding increasing invention. These visions can be extremely seductive to their creators, for they offer a liberating alternative to often difficult personal circumstances, providing stimulation, satisfaction, and a sense of accomplishment and control that they may lack in their everyday lives. Some may become immersed in their fantasy, choosing it over the reality of day-to-day living; others may be simultaneously able to participate in both their fantasy and reality, retaining the ability to distinguish between the two and moving between them at will.

Creators of such alternative constructs may be secretive about them, for fear of being labeled eccentric or even insane by observers familiar with popularized theories about mental illness. Yet such fantasies are intriguing to the outside observer, because conventional elements may take on strange characteristics therein. On rare occasions, a creator will be motivated to share an alternative reality with others through words or images, abstracting his or her mental excitement through artistic expression.[1] The ensuing feeling of (at least momentary) satisfaction seems to be common to all artists; the so-called Outsider Artist appears to be distinguished from the cultural and social mainstream by a compulsive preoccupation with his or her personalized and idiosyncratic alternate reality.[2]

Although such obsessions may merely reflect a self-absorbed eccentricity, they may also be evidence of more severe mental disturbances; the question of these correlations has been researched and discussed for well over a century. Contemporary cultural critics, from Susan Sontag

to Sander Gilman, have cautioned that the forms and significance of both creativity and mental illness adjust to the conventions of each time and culture;[3] consequently, certain artists of the past who were diagnosed as "mad" would not be judged so today. Psychiatrist Kay Redfield Jamison of the Johns Hopkins School of Medicine, among others, characterizes the current scholarship, which perceives a continuum with acute psychosis at one end and the moody artistic temperament at the other.

Since the complex, enigmatic work of A. G. Rizzoli was introduced to a limited public in 1990, art historians, theologians, psychiatrists, and artists – who have been encouraged, in part, by Rizzoli's own articulated descriptions of "mental disturbances" – have pondered its characteristics in an attempt to classify Rizzoli's mental state. However, posthumous "diagnoses" of artists significantly limit our understanding of art that does not fit within traditional aesthetic or cultural norms. An in-depth study of Rizzoli's work challenges us to bridge the somewhat arbitrary constructs defining eccentricity and insanity, and to broaden the parameters of what we perceive to be art: neither the man nor his works fall neatly into any category.

Rizzoli's story is compelling: a lifelong bachelor who lived with his beloved mother, he was traumatized in his teens by his father's disappearance. Introverted, sexually repressed, and friendless, his personal circumstances were characterized by pain and powerlessness, stimulating a need to reorder and balance his life. Quietly and loyally laboring on mundane drafting work during the day, he spent his nights and weekends on a monumental yet secret task: the delineation of a new world, for which he served as "High Prince" and "Master Architect." Undertaken at the command of spiritual guides, these drawings and writings document a life lived, in his words, "in an unbelievable hermetically sealed, spherical, inalienable maze of light and sound, seeing imagery expanding in every direction . . . ."[4] Unprecedented in their richness and clarity, Rizzoli's art has been hailed by scholars as the "find of the century."

A. G. RIZZOLI. C. 1918. GELATIN SILVER PRINT, 6 9/16 x 4 9/16" (16.7 x 11.6 CM). PHOTOGRAPHER UNKNOWN. COLLECTION THE ESTATE OF THE ARTIST

MOTHER STANDING IN FRONT OF
PEACH TREE. 1934. GELATIN
SILVER PRINT. 4⅛ X 2⅜"
(10.5 X 6 CM). COLLECTION
THE ESTATE OF THE ARTIST

The parents of Achilles G. Rizzoli, Innocente Rizzoli and Erminia (Emma) Dadami, were born in the culturally and linguistically Italian (Romansch) areas of southern Switzerland.[5] Innocente immigrated to the United States in 1885; Emma arrived four years later. Details of their meeting and brief courtship remain unknown; after marrying in 1890, they settled near Pt. Reyes, in western Marin County, north of San Francisco, where Innocente worked on a dairy ranch. Young Achilles, born in 1896, was the fourth of five children, and had an apparently unremarkable childhood as a member of this poor immigrant family. In 1912, he moved to Oakland to study at the Polytechnic College of Engineering; in 1913, his oldest sister, Olympia, became pregnant out of wedlock and, in disgrace, left Marin to join Achilles in Oakland, accompanied by Emma and the other children. Innocente remained behind at the dairy, and the family never lived together again; in spring 1915 Innocente disappeared with a gun stolen from his employer. This event traumatized nineteen-year-old Achilles, and he memorialized it in later drawings as a proposed building titled "The Dark Horse of the Festival Year."[6]

Olympia married the father of her baby in 1914, but they never lived together and filed for divorce a year later. She and her daughter remained in Oakland, while Emma's three younger children moved with their mother to San Francisco. (Oldest brother Rinaldo, the "black sheep" of the family, went off on his own during this time and was never heard from again.) Between 1915 and 1933, the remaining members of the Rizzoli family moved at least seven times to various places in the Mission District and Bernal Heights; in the interim, too, siblings Alfred and Palmira both married and moved away from home. By mid-1933, Achilles and his mother resettled for the last time, in a modest four-room cottage in a working-class neighborhood on Alabama Street, where he was to live for the rest of his life. Achilles, or A. G., as he later preferred to be known, made few friends and never married; he shared the single bedroom in the house with his mother, and his writings reveal that he remained a lifelong virgin.[7]

GROUP VIEW ADJOINING 1668
ALABAMA ST. 1934. GELATIN
SILVER PRINT, 2½ X 4¼"
(6.4 X 10.8 CM). COLLECTION
THE ESTATE OF THE ARTIST

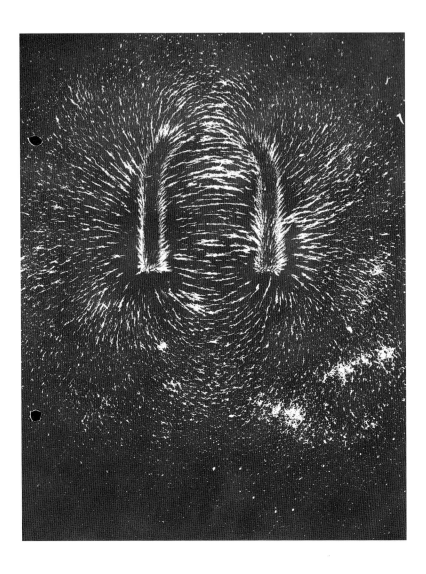

SINGLE HORSESHOE MAGNET.
c. 1913-14. PHOTOGRAM
ON BLUEPRINT PAPER, 11 X
8½" (27.9 X 21.6 CM).
COLLECTION THE ESTATE OF
THE ARTIST

THIS SHEET FROM RIZZOLI'S
SCHOOL NOTEBOOK SHOWS AN
EXERCISE FOR HIS ELEMENTARY
ELECTRICITY AND MAGNETISM
CLASS AT THE POLYTECHNIC
COLLEGE OF ENGINEERING IN
OAKLAND. THIS IMAGE REVEALS
A MARKED SIMILARITY WITH
SOME OF THE GRAPHICS HE
USED LATER TO ILLUSTRATE HIS
HEAVENLY DIALOGUES.

While at the Polytechnic College from 1912 to 1915, Rizzoli took classes such as mechanics, geometry, electrical engineering, and magnetism. His exercise notebook from school shows that he routinely received As and Bs on his work, wrote precisely, and tried hard to be a good student. Even at this early stage, his interest in architecture was evident, and he used his English assignments to explore subjects such as construction, drafting, and inventions.

During these years, the San Francisco Bay Area was steeped in images of a utopia generated by architecture. The 1906 earthquake and fire had sparked energetic efforts to revitalize San Francisco, and its victorious rebirth was symbolized by the grandiose optimism of the Panama-Pacific International Exposition of 1915. Given his early interests, it is no wonder that Rizzoli would pursue a career inspired by the heroic efforts of architects not only to rebuild the city but to define its cultural future.

In mid-1916 he was recommended for membership in the San Francisco Architectural Club, a private alternative to the limited university programs then available. This afforded him the opportunity to take such vocationally directed classes as mechanical drafting, rendering, and life-drawing; in the latter, his instructors introduced classical Greek theories about proportional relationships between architecture and the human body. The SFAC administration promoted numerous social events in which the students could interact with potential patrons, but as socializing was never easy for Rizzoli, it appears he did not partake of these events nor the nightclub scenes and boozy informality of the celebrated 1920s that many of his fellow students enjoyed. Rizzoli resigned his SFAC membership in 1923.

Although his school notebooks reveal an earnest boy trying to do well,[8] by the early 1920s he was beginning to sense that life would not live up to his expectations. A series of letters regarding two lawsuits that he initiated, one concerning a perceived "injustice" done to the family name by Olympia's ex-husband, and a second alleging breach of promise by a doctor who reneged on marrying his mother, reveal his frustrations on behalf of his family. Other papers describe his "invention" of the internal combustion engine, for which he felt someone else had taken the credit (and, of course, the economic gain).[9] "Injustice has been done me . . . ," he wrote in a later letter appealing a layoff, ill-conceived, he believed, because he was supporting his ailing mother,[10] who never left the house except to garden. A portrait emerges of a young man who felt unjustly abused by the world, and who was unable to get satisfaction from his repeated attempts to redress those circumstances. An increasing feeling of powerlessness permeates these documents.

Rizzoli worked at a variety of jobs during these early years, primarily in drafting, but also doing odd jobs, housework, and perhaps even typing. He was "compelled to labor 8, 9, or 10 hours daily . . . in order to earn the money to meet [m]y monthly obligations," he complained;[11] he may have been on welfare during the Depression years as well. In the early 1920s, his income tax returns show annual salaries up to the low $2,000s, but in 1928 there was a dramatic change, with earned income reduced to $51. He attached a note to this tax return that read, "The absence of income reported is due to the fact that I have during the past year directed my attention to literature[,] attempting poetry writing in particular[,] but none of my material has, as yet, proved saleable."[12]

His first ambitious creative endeavors, undertaken from 1927 to 1933, were a series of novellas and short stories featuring the utopian efforts of a group of idealistic architects. Verbose, stiff, and boring, each manuscript was rejected in turn by the various magazine publishers to whom it was submitted; in his files he kept all 280 rejection notices[13] as well as each methodically typed-out text. Next, under the name Peter Metermaid, Rizzoli tried self-publishing his text *The Colonnade* (aka *Colonnaded Plaza*). His only effort to be published in any form, it was neither marketed nor distributed, and the three thousand copies remained wrapped and stored in his home. This novel introduced the fictional hero Vincent Reamer, who was "afraid of maids but unafraid of colonnades,"[14] a description that fit Rizzoli's life as well.

Frustrated by the lack of positive response to his literary works but still inspired by utopian fantasies, in 1935

Rizzoli shifted to producing large pen-and-ink renderings of architectural designs. Utopian images are found throughout the history of visionary architecture, but Rizzoli's elaborate buildings were unusual in that most were symbolic representations ("transfigurations," in his words) of people he knew, intended to glorify a heavenly world of his own creation. He later referred to his works from the period 1935–44 by the acronym SYMPA, each letter designating a separate category of drawings. S stood for the Symbolization drawings, some two dozen large renderings of classic-style buildings, each of which symbolized a family member, acquaintance, or event. Y referred to the Y.T.T.E. series (pronounced it-ty), an acronym for "Yield To Total Elation," being a half-dozen plot plans delineating a symbolic world exposition. M represented Miscellaneous lists, signs, and poems. P were the PIA drawings, short for *piafore* (itself an invented word referring to the common pinafore dresses worn by the young girls in his neighborhood), including buildings and monuments in the Y.T.T.E., as well as portraits of those involved in it. A was Rizzoli's Amplification of these four categories of drawings in the *Achilles Tectonic Exhibit Portfolio*, in which he recorded and interpreted his work to date.

The first drawing in the Symbolization series, appropriately enough, was *Mother Symbolically Represented/ The Kathredal*, a combination birthday card, full-scale drawing honoring and symbolizing the strength, beauty, and spiritualism of his mother, and premiere structure in the Y.T.T.E. world exposition. Many of the Symbolization buildings are described on the drawings themselves as "heavenly homes" or "heavenly inheritances," meant to symbolize an actual metamorphosis of the person following death, as well as an architectural personification of their essential attributes. At times these terms referred to the physical being (". . . blood, flesh and bone converted into an/inheritance of stone-hard elegance . . .");[15] other times he wrote of "the conversion of the soul into objects of monumental character."[16]

The concept of the metamorphosis of humans into stone or other hard material has many precedents in Western literary and oral traditions, from Medusa and King Midas in the Greek myths, to folktales in which beautiful

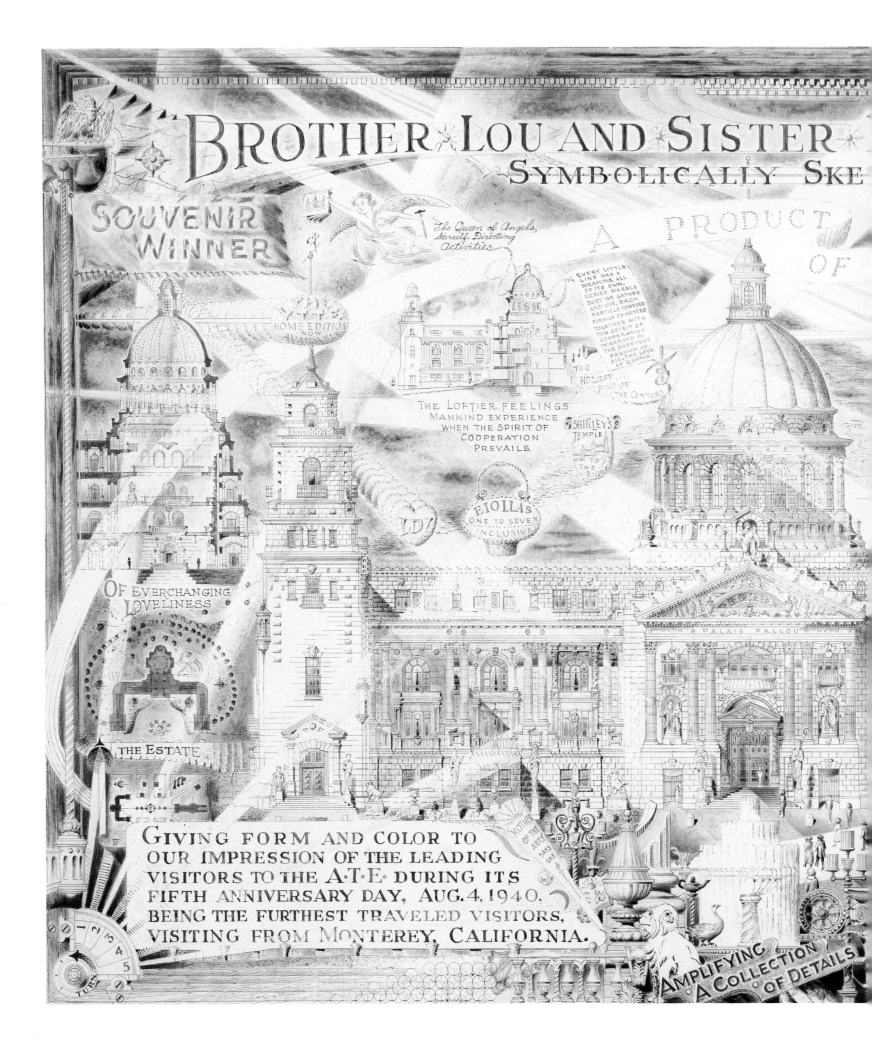

BROTHER LOU AND SISTER
PALMIRA LIEVRE SYMBOLICALLY
SKETCHED/PALAIS PALLOU.
1941. INK ON RAG PAPER,
25¾ X 35¾" (65.4 X 90.8 CM).
COLLECTION THE AMES GALLERY,
BERKELEY

maidens or handsome princes suffer enchantment by an evil sorcerer, to the biblical inhabitants of Sodom and Gomorrah. In contrast, Rizzoli's transfiguration of people into stone was based not on fear, punishment, or subjugation, as in the myths and tales, but on admiration. Those who were so honored were his heroes: family members, neighbors who appreciated him or his work, fellow members or priests of his church, and exalted historical figures.

The meticulously crafted drawings for this rapidly developing imaginary world combined Beaux-Arts architectural idioms[17] with an eclectic borrowing of Roman, Renaissance, Baroque, Art Deco, and Art Nouveau styles. Spectacular lighting displays reminiscent of a Hollywood premiere (but probably more specifically referential to the lighting for the Panama-Pacific Exposition),[18] as well as more populist elements of commercial advertising

and P. T. Barnum were also added.[19] This fusion of styles,[20] many of which Rizzoli had probably seen only in books, was a juxtaposition not many could have successfully presented without parody. Such satire would have been unthinkable to him, however, given his self-assigned title of "earthly architectural assistant and transcriber" to God. Proud of the grand design of his work, Rizzoli described it as an "Expeau of Magnitude, Magnificence and Manifestation."[21]

His drawing technique followed the elaborate Beaux-Arts system, which was predicated upon numerous draft concepts and detail sketches; however, although Rizzoli was a prodigious accumulator, with books, lists, newspapers, letters, and other documents found among his effects, no extant sketches were found that might have shed additional light on the development of the Symbolization drawings. Close examination of these drawings reveals little trace of preliminary graphite outlines; his penned lines are sure and steady, and his detailing is tight and compulsive. His notes, frequently recorded on the drawings themselves, did not elaborate on his processes or procedures, but indicated that a single rendering would often require several months of devoted labor. Though a small man, some of the drawings Rizzoli made were almost as large as he was: the largest approach five by three feet.

Rizzoli always desired a public audience to appreciate his creative efforts. To this end, beginning in 1935, he set aside the first Sunday in August as an open house for the presentation of the evolving SYMPA drawings. He arranged a "gallery" in the front room of his house for the "Achilles Tectonic Exhibit" (the A.T.E.); his 1940 *Portfolio* documented a floor plan and elevations of the walls indicating how he had installed the drawings. To advertise, he put up hand-lettered signs around the neighborhood, but aside from some of the local children, only two coworkers and a few relatives ever attended this annual display. Those who did were honored with future architectural symbolizations, although most of his subjects never knew about nor saw them. Rizzoli hosted the A.T.E. openings for five more years without increased attendance; although he discontinued the public exhibitions after 1940, he honored

A.T.E. Colleague 1935/
Accepted Emblem Design.
1939. Ink on rag paper,
7 x 8" (17.8 x 20.3 cm).
Collection The Ames Gallery,
Berkeley

ACHILLES TECTONIC STUDIO
EXHIBIT ROOM
=OF=
DECORATIVE
ARCHITECTURE
DELINEATION
PREPARED BY THE CURATOR
.10¢ ADMISSION   PAYMENT EXPECTED BEFORE ENTE,
FOUNDED ON A MONEY-BACK POLI(
HOURS 1 TO 5 P.M.   A.G. RIZZOLI, CURATO
INAUGURATED JULY 1,1935

ACHILLES TECTONIC STUDIO.
1935. INK ON RAG PAPER, 8⅛ X
10½" (20.7 X 26.7 CM).
COLLECTION THE AMES GALLERY,
BERKELEY

ACHILLES TECTONIC EXHIBIT.
C. 1935. INK ON PAPER, 18 X 24"
(45.7 X 61 CM). COLLECTION
THE AMES GALLERY, BERKELEY

ACHILLES
TECTONIC
EXHIBIT
ADMISSION .10c
HOURS 1 TO 5 P.M.

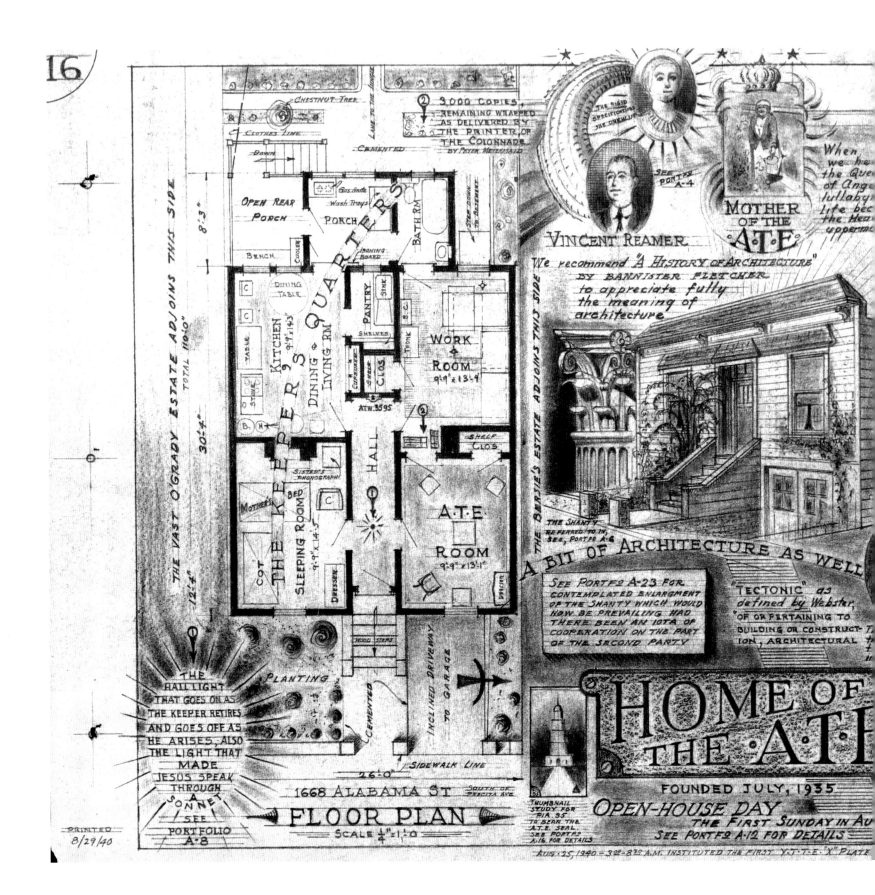

CHESTNUT TREE

3.000 COPIES, REMAINING WRAPPED AS DELIVERED BY THE PRINTER OF THE COLONNADE BY PETER MEDONALD

CLOTHES LINE

CEMENTED

DOWN

MOTHER OF THE ·A·T·E·

OPEN REAR PORCH

PORCH

Gas Grate
Wash Trays

BATH RM

STEP DOWN TO BASEMENT

VINCENT REAMER

BENCH

COOLER

IRONING BOARD

We recommend "A History of Architecture"
BY BANNISTER FLETCHER
to appreciate fully
the meaning of
architecture

DINING TABLE

PANTRY

SINK

C

TABLE

SHELVES

S.C.

C

CUPBOARD

WORK ROOM
9'9" x 13'9"

SHELF CLOS

STOVE

TRUNK

THE ·KEEPER'S· QUARTERS·

DINING & LIVING RM

ATW. 3595

2

B. H.

THE SHANTY REFERRED TO IN, SEE PORTFO A-6

A BIT OF ARCHITECTURE AS WELL

SISTER'S PHONOGRAPH

HALL

C

SHELF CLOS

MOTHER'S BED

A·T·E·

ROOM
9'9" x 13'1"

SEE PORTFO A-23 FOR CONTEMPLATED ENLARGMENT OF THE SHANTY WHICH WOULD NOW BE PREVAILING HAD THERE BEEN AN IOTA OF COOPERATION ON THE PART OF THE SECOND PARTY

"TECTONIC" as defined by Webster, "OF OR PERTAINING TO BUILDING OR CONSTRUCT-ION, ARCHITECTURAL

COT

SLEEPING ROOM
9'9" x 14'5"

DRESSER

DRESSER

WOOD STEPS

PLANTING

INCLINED DRIVEWAY TO GARAGE

HOME OF THE ·ATE·

THE HALL LIGHT THAT GOES ON AS THE KEEPER RETIRES AND GOES OFF AS HE ARISES; ALSO THE LIGHT THAT MADE JESUS SPEAK THROUGH A SONNET SEE PORTFOLIO A·8

CEMENTED

SIDEWALK LINE

THUMBNAIL STUDY FOR PIA 35 TO BEAR THE A.T.E. SEAL SEE PORTFO A-16 FOR DETAILS

FOUNDED JULY, 1935

OPEN-HOUSE DAY
THE FIRST SUNDAY IN AU

SEE PORTFO A-12 FOR DETAILS

26'-0"

1668 ALABAMA ST

SOUTH OF PRECITA AVE

FLOOR PLAN
SCALE 1/4"=1'-0"

PRINTED 8/29/40

AUG. 25, 1940 - 3:00-8:30 A.M. INSTITUTED THE FIRST Y.T.T.E. "X" PLATE

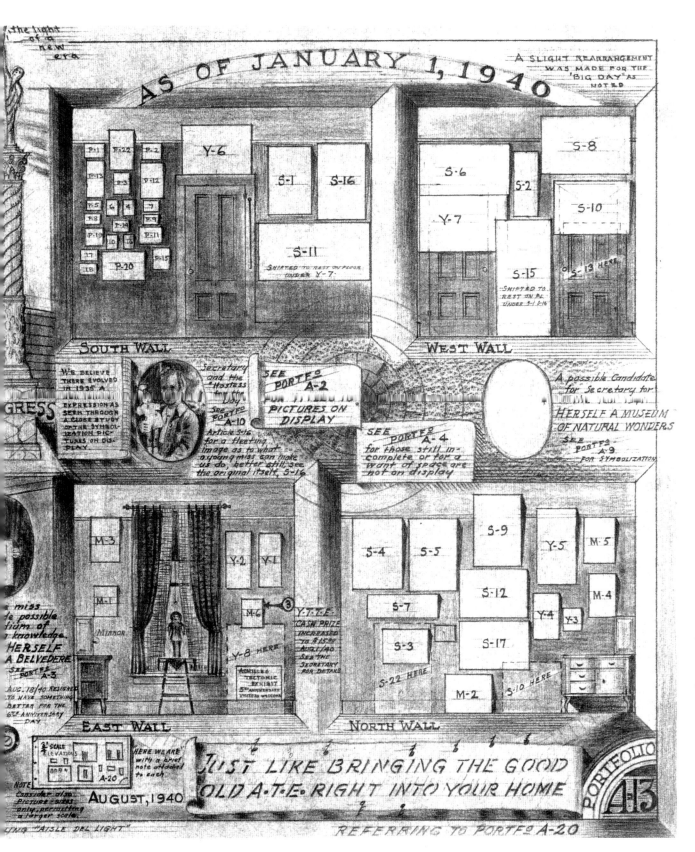

A.T.E. PORTFOLIO — A-13.
1940. DIAZO PRINT ON PAPER,
18 X 34" (45.7 X 86.4 CM).
COLLECTION THE AMES GALLERY,
BERKELEY

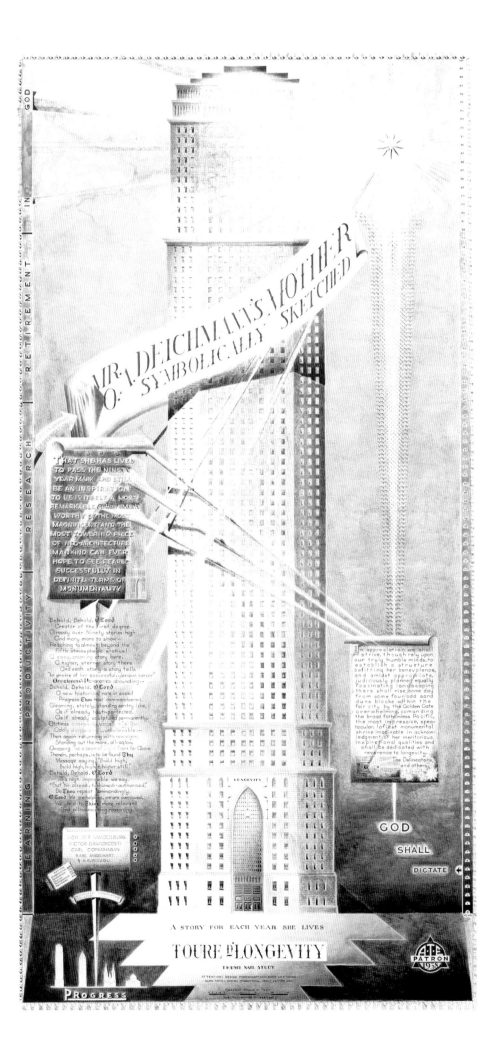

MR. O. A. DEICHMANN'S MOTHER
SYMBOLICALLY SKETCHED/
TOURE D'LONGEVITY. 1938. INK
ON RAG PAPER, 59 X 29"
(149.9 X 73.7 CM). COLLECTION
THE AMES GALLERY, BERKELEY

the A.T.E.'s anniversary in later writings, and left the drawings on display in his front room for the rest of his life. Rizzoli was clearly proud of his work: "Nothing Like It Ever Before Attempted," he proclaimed on one of his drawings.

The year 1936 was pivotal for Rizzoli. Local events such as the dedication of the San Francisco Bay Bridge and the groundbreaking for the 1939 Golden Gate International Exposition at Treasure Island must have stimulated his own utopian visions. This was also the year that he joined Otto A. Deichmann's small architectural firm as a draftsman, working in a windowless room for $1.50 an hour, a steady if not satisfying position he was to hold until his retirement almost forty years later.[22] According to his coworkers, Rizzoli was a conscientious and diligent although quiet and uncommunicative worker, devoted to his kindly and rather paternalistic employer.[23] Rizzoli, who had lost his father at a young age, must have cherished this relationship.[24]

Then, in late summer, twenty-one years after the disappearance of Rizzoli's father, the family was rocked by the news of the discovery of Innocente's deteriorated bodily remains in a deeply wooded section of Marin County, the result of an apparent suicide. That same year, Rizzoli's mother was hospitalized for gangrene, a complication from diabetes that resulted in the amputation of her leg. She never recovered, and died January 8, 1937, at the age of sixty-three. Rizzoli handled the funeral arrangements, and was remembered by a neighbor standing at his mother's open casket, trying to open her eyes.

Her death, following so closely upon the trauma of identifying his father's body, struck him hard. In 1936 he made her an elaborate Mother's Day card (a 28 by 48-inch drawing, "a work of art worthy of display in any art gallery"[25]), and continued to do so for several more years, each time symbolically depicting her as an ornate and majesterial Gothic-style cathedral.[26] These drawings later evolved into sonnets and prose, as each years' anniversary, birthday, and Mother's Day spurred Rizzoli to elaborate on his love and grief.[27]

Nor did he change their house from the way she had left it: he kept her nighttime "honey bucket" underneath her bed; her bonnet, boots, and corset in the closet and dresser.[28] He slept on a cot at the foot of her bed as he had while she lived, and continued to do so for more than thirty years after her death, leaving her empty bed untouched.[29] His family recalled that, always a quiet man who spoke only when spoken to, Rizzoli became even more withdrawn and introverted after his mother's death; his coworkers were told he "went to pieces."[30] Rizzoli took a grim pleasure in his asceticism, noting, for example, his habitual early rising and his frugal morning breakfast ("the same menu prevailing several years now"[31]). He spent little money on food and less on clothes, preferring instead to purchase art supplies with his meager wages. His life outside of Deichmann's firm became absorbed more and more by mental visions of elaborate buildings and his efforts to translate them to paper.

Neighbors rarely saw him, except for his almost ritual coming and going from work or from mass at St. Anthony's Church, small and silent in his conservative black suit. He paid all his bills in cash, keeping the change and every receipt for every purchase he ever made in envelopes stashed in boxes around his home. His home was slowly deteriorating around him: a hole appeared in the roof, vines covered the front of the house and protruded through the walls, piles of newspaper and cat refuse surrounded him. Because of the vines, neighbors never saw any lights on in the house at night, so the children thought the house was haunted.[32]

The Kathredal
EAST ELEVATION
THE 1ST 20 YEARS.

GATEMAN
JOHONOR
INFORMANT

MOTHER

SYMBOLICALLY

BIRTHDAY GREETINGS NOV. 11, 1936.

REPR

A Picture of My Beautiful, Beautiful M

RATING
SYMBOLIZATION — 90%
COMPOSITION — 75%
DRAFTSMANSHIP — 50%
RENDERING — 40%

SENTED

ther

CARPPITTAN, GRANDICOSTI
AND COPANHAGEN, DELS.
REQUESTED BY A.G. RIZZOLI

MOTHER SYMBOLICALLY
REPRESENTED/THE KATHREDAL.
1936. INK ON RAG PAPER,
27¾ x 47⅝" (70.5 x 121 CM).
COLLECTION THE AMES GALLERY,
BERKELEY

PAINTED BY THE SUN. 1939.
INK ON RAG PAPER, 30 x 18"
(76.2 x 45.7 CM). COLLECTION
THE AMES GALLERY, BERKELEY

Rizzoli seemed oblivious to all this; although in his writings he occasionally commented on the degradation of his physical surroundings, he made it clear that his energies were concentrated on the exquisite heavenly domain that would follow this earthly "saddening well of tears."[33] He did not fear death; rather, he pragmatically acknowledged it ("One more day, one step closer to the grave"), and actually welcomed it not only as deliverance from his labors, but also as the time when he would claim his own heavenly inheritance that memorialized his good works while "tarrying on the surface of the earth." Heaven, he felt, was "not a place for the dead only, but the center of the Universe of constantly expanding activities."[34]

Rizzoli's buildings, created to grace this life after death, were illustrations of his own creed about beauty, stature, and importance, and also of his fervent belief that they were God-given ideals, represented by the kind of buildings he imagined would be in paradise. Exact standards of proportion defined by what the Beaux-Arts school determined were universally correct "laws" of harmony, symmetry, and balance infused his works, while contemporary canons of architectural "character" (through which buildings could manifest human characteristics and even emotions[35]) inspired him to imbue his drawings with the personal attributes of his acquaintances. It is also likely that Rizzoli portrayed his acquaintances as buildings because he possessed the talent to do so; his portraits, in contrast, were amateurish and clumsy, and his writings generally turgid and at times incomprehensible.

Rizzoli favored the Renaissance concept of the architect as a humanist practicing the liberal arts,[36] as well as the later characterization of architecture as the proponent and portraitist of civilization.[37] Much taken with such expansive views of the architect's mandate, he was inspired by theorists such as Frederic Le Play, who distilled this mandate to three elements: "the place, the work, and the people."[38]

These elements are recalled in Rizzoli's 1943 drawings *The Place*, *The Job*, and *The Man*, where he distilled his grand utopian efforts to their core: detailing a map showing the location of the imaginary island upon which his social vision was constructed, a block plan indicating the

THE MAN. 1943. INK ON RAG PAPER, 9 X 6⅛" (22.9 X 15.6 CM). COLLECTION THE AMES GALLERY, BERKELEY

A GREATER GREATNESS IN THE MAKING

THE "SAYANPEAU"
MEANING
"WAIT A MOMENT"
OF, APPARENTLY, HIS DERIVATION

IRWIN PETER SICOTTE, JR
SYMBOLICALLY DELINEATED
IN REVEREND ADMIRATION FOR
THE INTELLECTUAL BRILLIANCY
HE ALREADY POSSESSES

Irwin Peter Sicotte, Jr.
Symbolically Delineated/
The "Sayanpeau." 1936. Ink
on rag paper, 35⅛ x 23½"
(89.9 x 59.7 cm). Collection
The Ames Gallery, Berkeley

major components of the exposition, and a portrait of Y.T.T.E.'s "founder," Vincent Argent Reamer.[39] In this paradise, asceticism and belief in God eliminated the social ills resulting from the carnal and worldly existence on earth, so Rizzoli apparently found no need to propose hospitals, prisons, or other such structures common to most "civilized" societies. In general, the kind of proletarian lifestyle that Rizzoli himself led was basically ignored in this schema, as were the needs of the lower social classes; this may have been the purposeful result of delegating the determination of the needs of "the people" to fictional architect Reamer, an alter-ego,[40] thus effectively replacing them in Rizzoli's trinity of essential elements.

Rizzoli's technical background gave him a familiarity with pictorial and emblematic insignia such as that found in legal or ceremonial documents; he must have felt they lent authority and validity to his labors by their inclusion, and he used them liberally in his drawings. They contrasted with the unusual mix of emotional, witty, and quasi erotic commentary that encircled the central building images, and served on another level to distance Rizzoli from his subject and his audience, thus reinforcing his personal tendency to withdraw from human relationships. The embellished commentary – unconventional and unusual in architectural renderings – signifies that although at casual glance these drawings appear to be bona fide architectural renderings of buildings that could have been built, they were actually symbols that through metaphor, allegory, and pun simultaneously beckon and exclude us from his private world.

Despite the seriousness of his goal, Rizzoli's sense of humor is revealed through the names of his imaginary "collaborators" (for example, Victor Betterlaugh and John McFrozen), public sculpture (such as *The Sungkenart*, "commemorating the lost art of remaining virgin lifelong"), buildings (the "P.P.P." and the "A.S.S." were the bathrooms), and the ancillary titles, acronyms, puns, and comments lettered around borders in illuminated characters.

His humor is also revealed in *Shirley Jean Bersie Symbolically Sketched/Shirley's Temple*, an elaborate drawing that juxtaposed Rizzoli's classical "high art" objective with an obvious Hollywood reference, as he "symbolically sketched" six-year-old neighbor Shirley Jean Bersie. Rizzoli and four imaginary associates (the "Delineators") divided *Shirley's Temple* into four units, the first of which was "to be rushed to completion at once," with the others following at critical stages in her maturity: ages ten, sixteen (the "age of choosing"), and twenty-four, by which time he anticipated that she would be a *Kathredal*, i.e., a mother. Symbolization, composition, design, drafting, and rendering were graded on the work itself – as they would have been in a Beaux-Arts style classroom – garnering 90%, 75%, 50%, 50%, and 40% respectively. The rendering is also embellished with "Shirley Bersie's Song" (composed of two verses and a chorus), the official emblem of the A.T.E., memoranda such as "Love's Delightful Labors," a sidebar indicating that Shirley is "Hereby to be the First Lady of the Y.T.T.E.," and that the temple was "Requested by His Prince, a son of Jesus, First within the Heart of God."

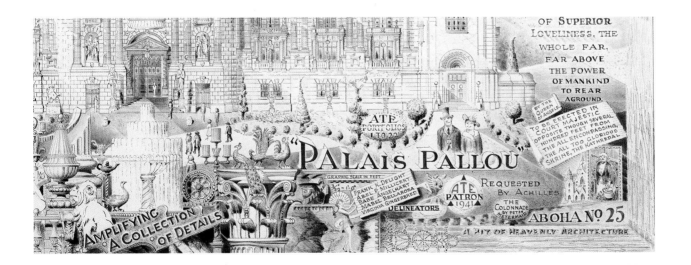

SHIRLEY'S TEMPLE

REQUESTED BY HIS PRINCE,
A SON OF JESUS
FIRST WITHIN
THE HEART
OF GOD

SHIRLEY BERSIE'S SONG

At six already telling princes how
To please the maiden quaintly fair
With eager hands and mind and sweat of brow
To us this seems divinely square:

Chorus:
Shirley Bersie is having a Temple made
In her behave, delightful all—
High, reaching to almost the sun, well weighed
With greens and shade and shadows tall,
With here and there the merry domes on
And each a touching story tells
In praise of her keen ways which we admire
That subtler boughs be made of belles.

At ten she shall tell lads galore to make
The best of time and strive the more
In manners virgin princes wide awake
And master super maidens fore:

A SWEETER SPIRIT IN
MANKIND'S UPLIFT SHIRLEY
BERSIE, AT 6, INSTITUTED

URGED, HEREBY TO BE THE
FIRST LADY OF THE Y.T.T.E.

OUR FONDEST HOPE
COMAKER OF

"LIKE AN ANGEL FROM HEAVEN"

LOVE'S
DELIGHTFUL
LABORS

SHIRLEY JEAN BERSIE
SYMBOLICALLY SKETCHED

IN DEEP APPRECIATION OF THE KINDLY INTEREST
SHE HAS SHOWN FOR THE A.T.E.

AS ON ONE DAY SHE RANG THE BELL,
SIGHING TENDERLY: "CAN I COME IN AND
SEE YOUR PICTURES". THIS TO GOD MEANT
"HEEDING NOBLY THE CALL OF THE BEAUTIFUL".
THEREUPON OUR ALMIGHTY LORD, CREATOR
OF THE FIRST DEGREE, MASTER ARCHITECT, AND
MASTER BUILDER, SPOKE WITH GRATITUDE.
"A GODDESS IN THE MAKING SHIRLEY BERSIE
SHALL BE FROM NOW ON, ON FOREVERMORE."

VON DER MAIDENBURG
VICTOR GRANDICOSTI
CARL COPANHAGAN
BABE ANGELHART
AND A.G. RIZZOLI
DELINEATORS

UNIT A
TO BE RUSHED
TO COMPLETION
AT ONCE

UNIT B
CONSTRUCTION
TO START WHEN
OUR POTENTIAL
ANGEL REACHES
THE BEAUTIFUL
AGE OF TEN

UNIT C
TO START WHEN OUR
MARBLE-LIKEN MAIDEN
REACHES THE AGE OF

UNIT D

UPON OUR WEARY, ACHING SHOULDERS
LORD GOD RESTED THE RESPONSIBILITY,
COMMANDING STOUTLY: "LET THERE BE NO THOUGHTS
OF PLEASURE NOR OF REST, LET THERE BE NOT THE
SLIGHTEST MOMENT OF NEGLIGENCE UNTIL SHIRLEY'S
TEMPLE IS REARED AND FUNCTIONING TO THE COMPLETE,
EXACTING SATISFACTION OF HIS HIGH PRINCE, THE VIRGIN."

PATRON
1939

Shirley's Temple, like Rizzoli's other designs, is an ambitious mixture of excessive ornamentation with an almost fanatic, formal regard for the classicism and precision of the architectural line. The rendering depicts an expansive Gothic tower built on a wide base, with side elements referencing a Roman coliseum and midlevel corner turrets that are rather moderne. Three successively larger vertical towers flank the front elevation, each topped with a lithe female figure (Shirley?), fronting a somewhat surreal landscaped garden filled with statues on pedestals, formal plantings, strolling pedestrians, and gawking sightseers. Soldiers outfitted in the style of Her Majesty's Royal Guard, complete with lofty headdresses and bemedaled uniforms, protect the sides and entrance to the temple. Intricate architectural details on roofs, window treatments, and the overall facade almost overshadow a small white figure that stands at one of the entrances to the temple, as it does in the entry of many of Rizzoli's buildings. This figure, a scale indicator, may also be a representation of Rizzoli himself, defining his authorship and protecting his creation.

Shirley and her girlfriends were some of Rizzoli's most communicative acquaintances, and he idealized them as muses as he had idealized his mother. He seemed particularly fond of Shirley, whom he made secretary and hostess of the A.T.E. (without her knowledge), dedicating to her not only the *Temple* but also poems describing her as an angel. He took snapshots of the neighborhood children, and Shirley appeared most often, at times with a toy rabbit or doll he gave her, other times holding up his drawings for him so he could document them.

Then, on April 12, 1936, his idealizations of femininity were challenged when he viewed female genitalia for the first time as a three-year-old neighborhood girl played next door. "Hold everything!" he wrote. "How the heart throbbed puzzlingly trying desperately to escape through . . . the tightening passage known as the throat . . . at the thought that at the old age of 40 one should finally get a glimpse of the veeaye . . ."[41] He had difficulty "interpreting the reactions experienced during that incomparable moment. . . . It was not until we [created] a piece of architecture . . . radically different did we regain our mental equilibrium." This became the symbolization drawing *The Primalglimse at Forty*, a huge phallic tower ornamented with his emblems for the male and female genitals (the male a phallic gargoyle; the female, or "barbin," classically urnlike) and densely annotated with his comments. From this time on he reveals his obsession with the child Virginia, (page 107)

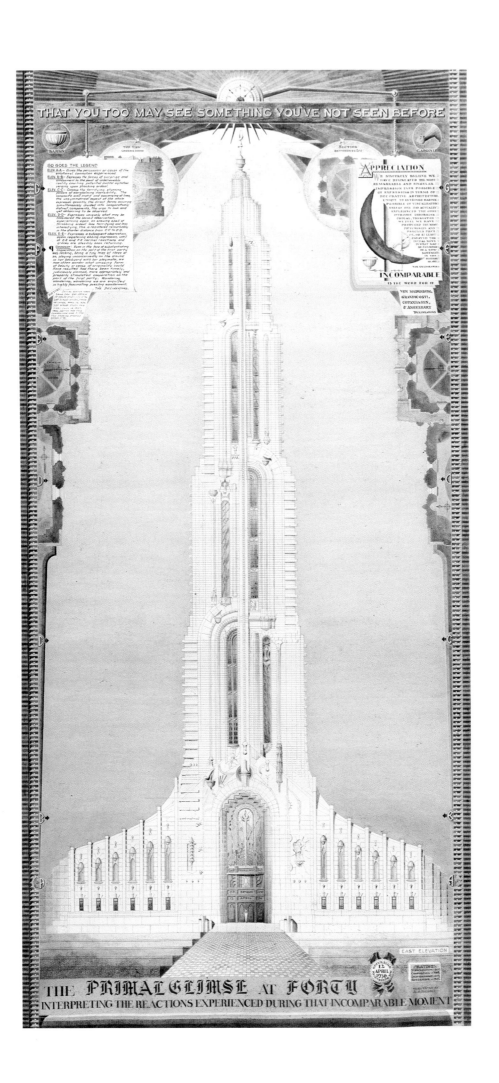

THE PRIMALGLIMSE AT FORTY.
1938. INK ON RAG PAPER,
54 X 26⅝" (137.2 X 67.6 CM).
COLLECTION THE AMES GALLERY,
BERKELEY

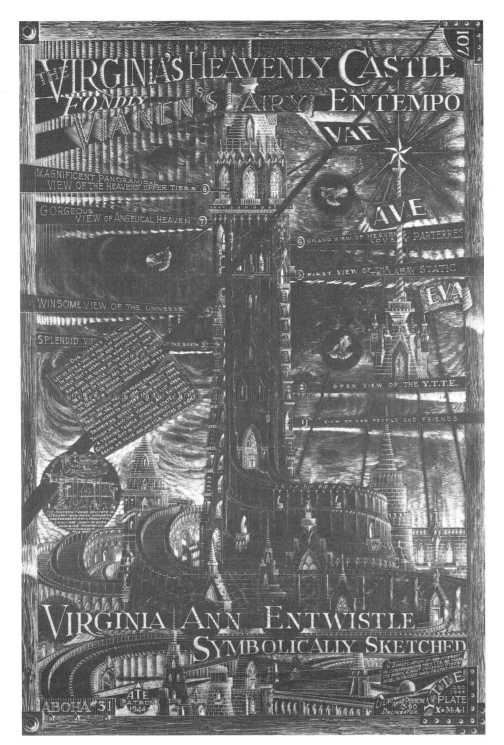

VIRGINIA ANN ENTWISTLE
SYMBOLICALLY SKETCHED/
VIRGINIA'S HEAVENLY CASTLE.
1944. BLUEPRINT ON PAPER,
36 X 24" (91.4 X 61 CM).
COLLECTION VIRGINIA
BAGATELOS AND THE AMES
GALLERY, BERKELEY

THE ORNAMENT. 1936. INK
ON RAG PAPER, 17⅞ X 8⅞"
(45.4 X 22.6 CM). PRIVATE
COLLECTION

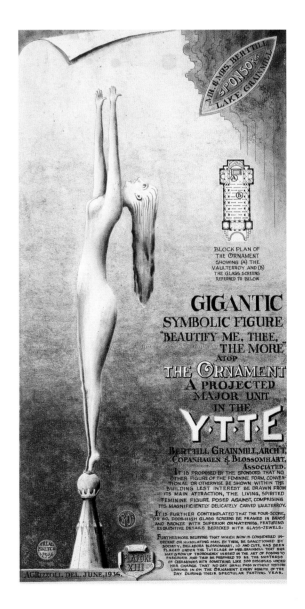

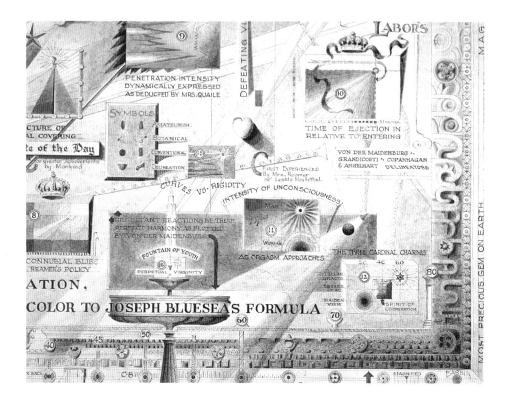

THE BLUESEA HOUSE (DETAIL).
1938. INK ON RAG PAPER,
20⅜ x 30⅜" (51.8 x 77.2 CM).
COLLECTION MICHAEL GROSSMAN,
NEW YORK

his neighbor, creating additional drawings to her such as *The Veeaye/The Ornament*, another towering building produced "that phallism may be revived," and vaunting "perpetual virginity for perpetual youth." Despite Rizzoli's manifest interest in both Virginia and Shirley, there is absolutely no evidence that his relationship with them overstepped any appropriate bounds; his desires to see the "feminine form" ("there's nothing as soothing than being accorded a view," he commented) were instead fulfilled by girlie pin-up calendars.[42]

Once engaged in exploring overtly sexual themes in his work, he continued with *The Bluesea House*, a 1938 drawing that charted the formula for sexual orgasm, symbolized and measured by a variety of graphs, diagrams, and gauges. The absurdity of a lifelong virgin delineating this concept was not lost on Rizzoli; Victor Betterlaugh, John McFrozen, and Von Der Maidenberg were acknowledged on the work for their counsel and observations, for it had only been two years before, at the age of forty, that Rizzoli had become informed about the sexual act:

ASKED BUT TACTFULLY IGNORED: A young girl . . . asked [me] in a most forward, sophisticated fashion, to "do it with her." Expressing ignorance and letting her chatter on, [she] described it coldly [and] somewhat shamefully, "he puts his into hers . . . ." Thus, on Sept. 9, 1940 we experienced a most amazing bit of comprehension far beyond belief.[43]

Such situations prompted occasional musing about marriage, although this was a fifth choice coming after such other options as "devote all time and energy to A.T.E. activities."[44] Although "marriage is not a state of perfect living," he wrote, "nevertheless it is better than experiencing that 'burning up' feeling day after day only to wither away wondering what is sex after all."[45]

Notwithstanding, the lure of a sexual experience was not sufficient to draw Rizzoli away from his life's work. As he continued to design and render new buildings, he concurrently developed a plot plan to situate the increasing number of structures constituting his utopian exposition, the Y.T.T.E. Modeled after the 1915 Panama-Pacific Exposi-

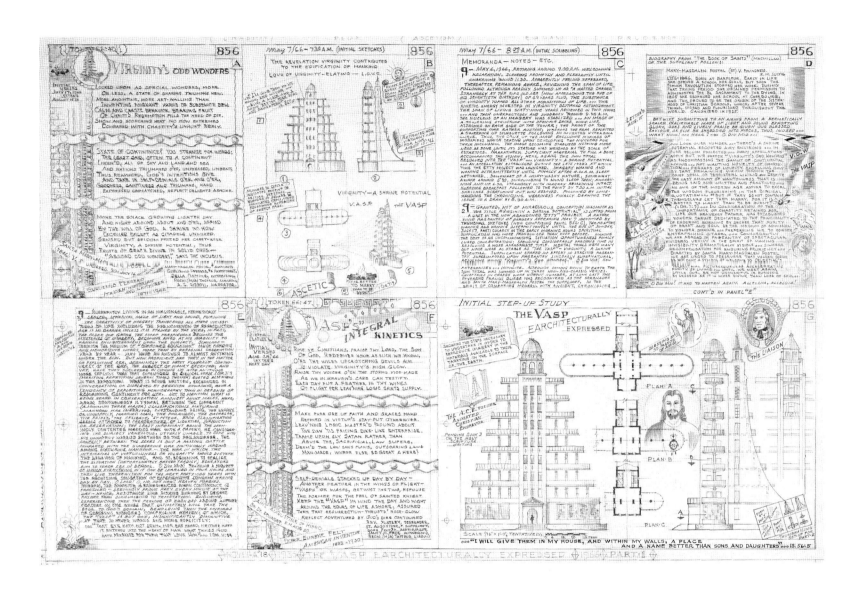

A.C.E. 408: NOVELLA #18
THE VASP EARCHITECTURALLY
EXPRESSED, PART 1. 1966.
GRAPHITE ON VELLUM, 24 x
36" (61 x 91.4 CM). COLLEC-
TION THE AMES GALLERY,
BERKELEY

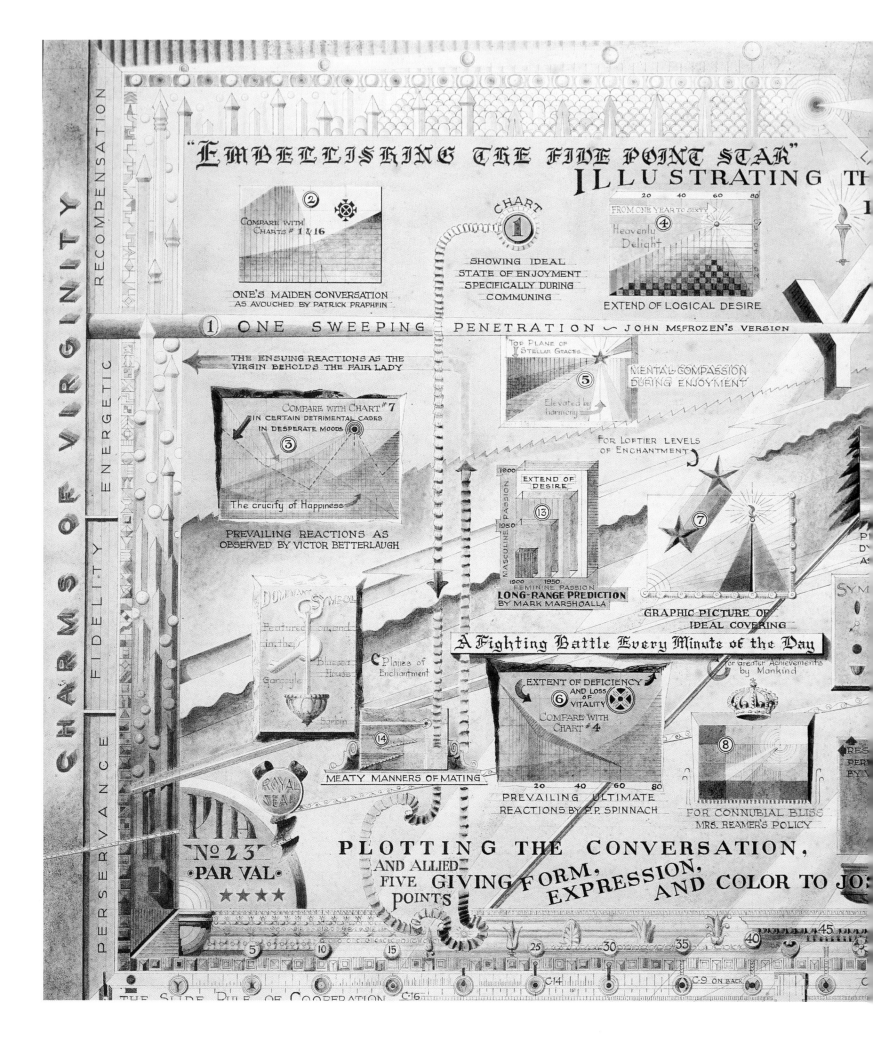

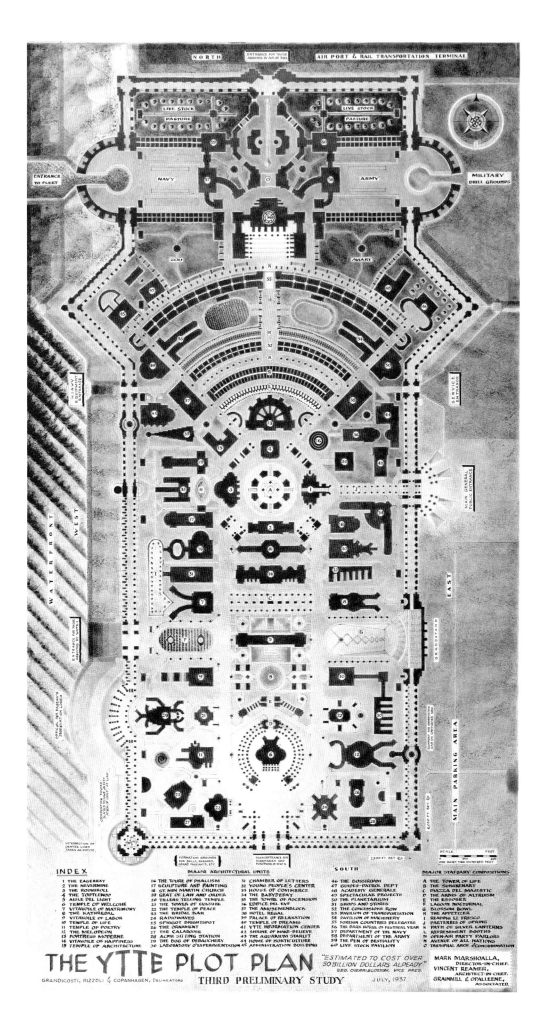

Y.T.T.E. ACCEPTED EMBLEM
DESIGN AND COLORS. 1939.
INK ON RAG PAPER, 7 X 8⅞"
(17.8 X 22.6 CM). COLLECTION
THE AMES GALLERY, BERKELEY

THE Y.T.T.E. PLOT PLAN —
FOURTH PRELIMINARY STUDY
KEY TO PLAN. 1938. INK ON RAG
PAPER, 24 X 13" (61 X 33 CM).
COLLECTION THE AMES GALLERY,
BERKELEY

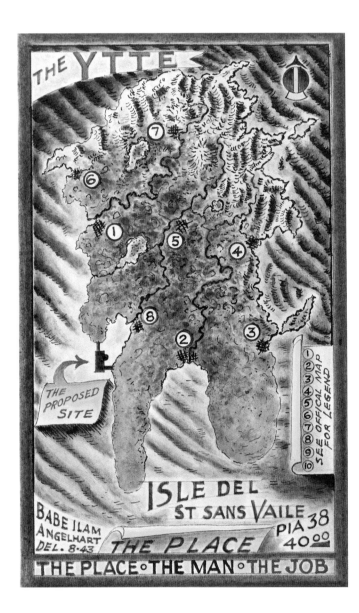

tion in San Francisco, the Y.T.T.E. plot plan also bears an intriguing resemblance to the floor plan of a cathedral. From 1935 to 1944 Rizzoli produced a half-dozen full revisions of the plot plan; even later, from 1958 to 1977, when he was concentrating on "transcribing" the third testament to the Bible in the A.C.E., he returned again and again to the Y.T.T.E., retracing and copying the plot plan, indicating revisions, redesigns, and additions. Yet he was ambivalent about his labors, writing that "from the beginning the Y.T.T.E. contemplation was a source of agony, of invisible things made visible by heavenly hosts projected upon the visible azure";[46] whereas elsewhere he commented about how fulfilling it was to do God's work. He compared himself to Saint Veronica of Umbria (1660–1727), who lived with almost continuous visions and revelations, yet was considered "practical and level-head[ed]"; he suggested that his "predicament" was similar to hers, and was indicative of the challenges he faced.[47] Despite the intensive labor and the emotional "ordeal" of his work, he acknowledged that it was fascinating, as well as a relief, "inasmuch as coming into the mind there should be a way of letting [the visions] out therefrom."[48]

With each incarnation, the number of structures included in the Y.T.T.E. exposition increased; by 1939, eighty separate building units were included, as well as twenty "Major Statuary Compositions." Despite his extensive work, however, he was still "haunted by an unsatisfied sense of rapture, there being 'so much to do, so little done,' . . . other [structures] equally noteworthy [need] to see the light of day in more vivid form than so far attempted, not to mention the numerous items dying in infancy or remaining buried in brain cells . . ."[49]

Although at first there was no reference to the specific location of the Y.T.T.E., later documents described and pictured it as an island complex. It is intriguing to note this with reference to the observations of author and art historian John MacGregor, who has remarked that

When an alternate world reaches [a certain] level of complexity and elaboration . . . , it often is relocated. . . . This tendency to relocate is frequently observed when the alter-

THE ROOMIROLL. 1940–43.
INK ON RAG PAPER, 7 X 8"
(17.8 X 20.3 CM). PRIVATE
COLLECTION, NEW YORK

THE EAGERRAY. 1939. INK
ON RAG PAPER, 5 X 8" (12.7 X
20.3 CM). PRIVATE COLLECTION,
NEW YORK

THE TOOTLEWOO. 1944. INK
ON RAG PAPER, 8 X 8" (20.3 X
20.3 CM). PRIVATE COLLECTION,
NEW YORK

THE NEVERMINE. 1944. INK
ON RAG PAPER, 5 X 15" (12.7
X 38.1 CM). PRIVATE COLLEC-
TION, NEW YORK

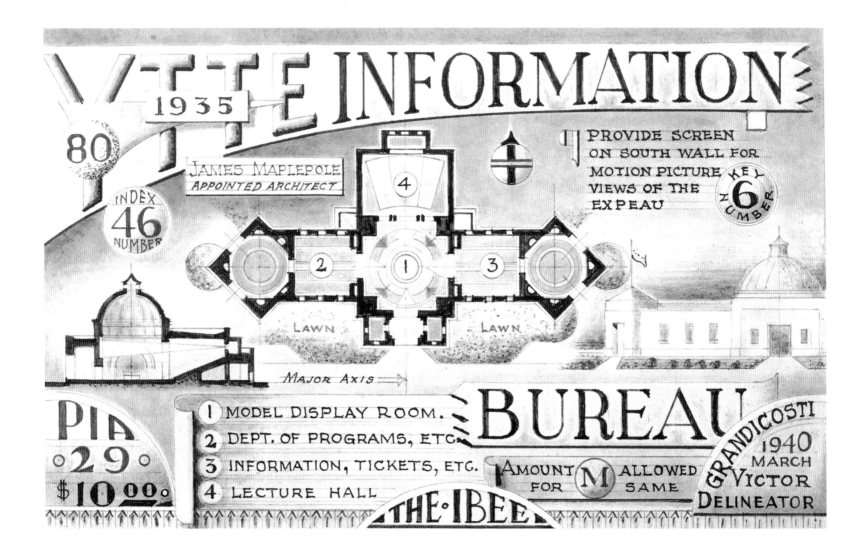

Y.T.T.E. INFORMATION BUREAU/
THE IBEE. 1940. INK ON RAG
PAPER, 5⅛ X 8" (13 X 30.3 CM).
COLLECTION THE AMES GALLERY,
BERKELEY

nate world becomes extremely personal and idiosyncratic, moving out beyond the conventional notion of a Christian paradise, with its traditional iconography, and assuming a pseudoscientific rather than a religious character.[50]

Rizzoli's Y.T.T.E. seems to suggest some of these elements.

On its secluded island – the shape of which, inverted, closely resembles the southern tip of Marin County – the Y.T.T.E. included a formal entrance court organized into seasonal quadrants, which he named the Eagerray (spring), Nevermine (summer), Roomiroll (autumn), and Tootle-woo (winter), a parody of the Court of the Four Seasons at the Panama-Pacific Exposition. The Y.T.T.E.'s borders were rimmed with esplanades, quays, and terraces, and entrances were carefully designed so that the "heavy equipment" and "service" entrances did not obstruct the

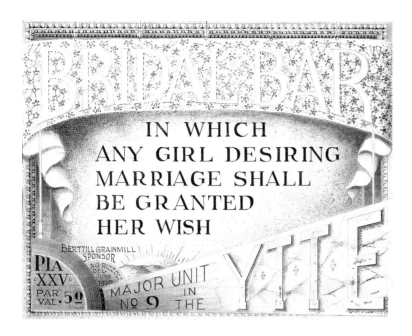

"main general public entrance." The northernmost areas of the Y.T.T.E. were protected by the military, beyond which were the airport and railway terminals. A sand beach, grandstand, aviary, and zoo were available for recreation, and "live stock pastures" were earmarked for grazing. Orienting structures such as the "Temple of Welcome" and the "Y.T.T.E. Information Bureau," centrally located along the main north/south axis, accentuated the symmetry and clarity of his overall plan as they directed visitors to their destinations.

In contrast to the previous full-scale symbolization "portraits" of specific family and friends, the Y.T.T.E. monumentalized such abstractions as labor, life, poetry, happiness, matrimony, culture, and peace. Other shrines in the Y.T.T.E. included the "Temple of Architecture," "The Toure of Phallism," the "Laboratory O'Experimentation," the "Palace of Relaxation," and the "Temple of Dreams." If one needed to use a rest room, there was the P.P.P. or the "Acme Sitting Station" (whose acronym was A.S.S.); if one wanted entertainment, a visit could be made to the "Shrine of Make Believe." When it was appropriate, visitors could find their way to *The Shaft of Ascension*, (page 79) "in which euthanasia is available to those desiring and meriting a pleasant, painless Bon Voyage from this land."

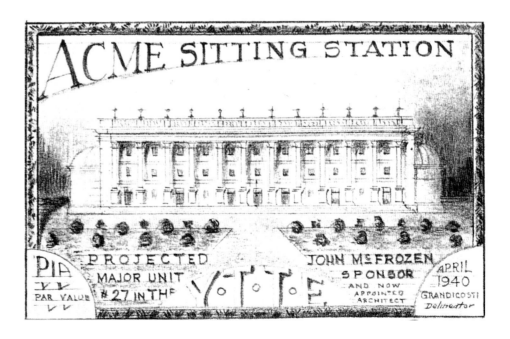

Although Rizzoli noted which structures were the tallest, there is a general sense that all of the units are equally important to the functioning and communicative intent of the Y.T.T.E. as a whole.[51]

The use of "maps" – such as these plot plans – is a fairly common pictorial device used to validate and organize alternate realities. Tibetan Buddhists have utilized mandalas as maps to a meditative reality; outsider artists such as Adolf Wölfli have used them as aesthetic expression; mainstream artists, including Bill Wiley and Jeremy Anderson, have parodied them. MacGregor has noted that in such a delineated universe, "description becomes more difficult, often impossible," and artists are "forced to invent new words to report experiences far beyond the norm. . . ."[52]

Rizzoli's acronyms, anagrams, word games, and invented vocabulary appear to validate this observation: "Not only words seldom used but new words are required," Rizzoli explained, as are "sounds superior to the best temporal music available . . . [in order] to understand . . . transfiguration properly. . . ."[53] The "Tokenquay," for example, was his own heavenly inheritance, a combination "screening center and archives in one."[54] The "Bipa Center" (aka Bill-Paying Center); "La Fane Haspine," or Temple

of Happiness; the "Biamtenet" shrine for St. Patrick; the "Akbaygem," Rufino M. Akbay's transfiguration; "Dae's Mae Maze," the projected home for the Apollo 11 astronauts; and so on, are all examples of his creation of new works identified by new words.[55] These new words are cumbersome, lacking rhythm or balance, yet are enigmatically evocative. At times the meaning of the building names can be deduced through their context or hints included in the commentary; at other times Rizzoli specifically explained them; still other names remained undefined, shrouded in the mystery of his invented vocabulary. Rather than using his new words to clarify his creations – the fundamental communicative function of language – Rizzoli's words instead emphasized the separation between himself and his audience; only he understood the meanings of his secret tongue. Rizzoli's words are not capriciously nonsensical; they are simply tied to a code that we cannot always break. He teases us with clues, but many are sufficiently obscure that one wonders if he really did want to divulge the details to an unknown public.[56]

The renderings of the Symbolization buildings and the full-scale Y.T.T.E. plot plans continued for nine years, until 1944. Then, from 1945 to 1957, Rizzoli worked on an illustrated prose narrative that included sketches for new architectural transfigurations and introduced themes that would be explored later in greater depth, such as his religious apparitions and a feminine embodiment of architecture. Unfortunately, only two sheets of the 207 believed to have been created during this period are extant.

Rizzoli experienced increasing numbers of visions from 1945 on; fully formed images of elaborate heavenly inheritances, they came to him at any and all times, day and night. He described them as multimedia "pageantry

MOTHER ANGELS PROEMSHAY-ING (DETAIL). 1941. INK ON RAG PAPER, 38 X 24" (96.5 X 61 CM). COLLECTION THE AMES GALLERY, BERKELEY

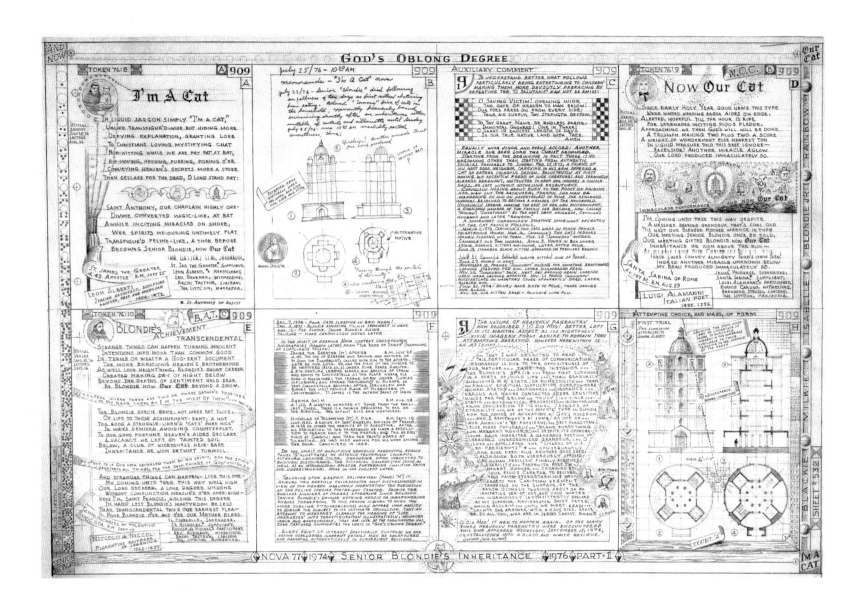

A.C.E. 352: NOVA 77 — SENIOR
BLONDIE'S INHERITANCE,
PART 1. 1976. GRAPHITE ON
VELLUM, 24 X 36" (61 X
91.4 CM). COLLECTION THE
AMES GALLERY, BERKELEY

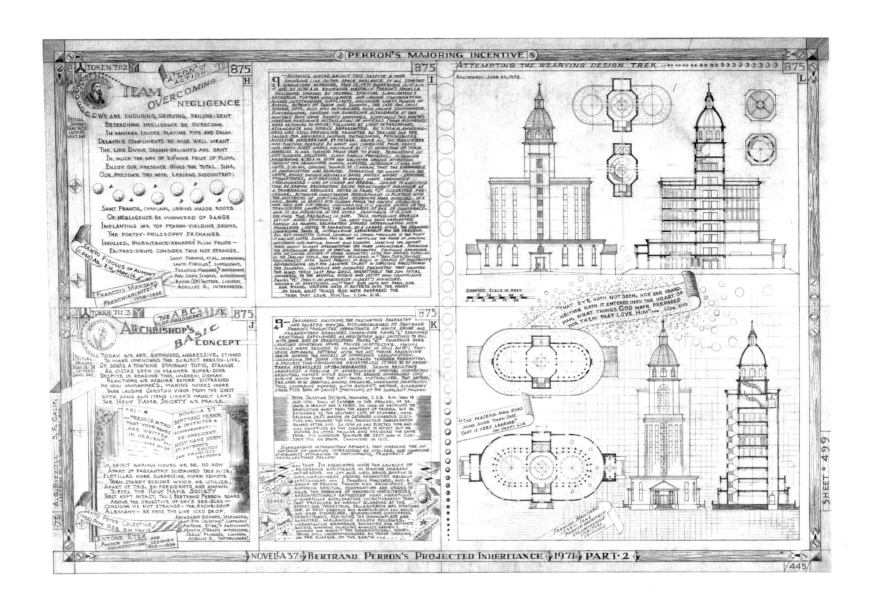

A.C.E. 499: NOVELLA 37 —
BERTRAND PERRON'S PROJECTED
INHERITANCE, PART 2. 1971.
GRAPHITE ON VELLUM, 24 × 36"
(61 × 91.4 CM). COLLECTION
THE AMES GALLERY, BERKELEY

in which action and drama and melodies and imagery . . . are . . . very much of the substance of air . . . [and] well nigh as essential."[57] He noted that others might experience "ear noises, headaches, sleepless nights" and interpret these disturbances as physical distress, but he believed them to be divine in nature and supernatural in origin.[58] He knew that such visions and voices were "held by many . . . [to be] controversial, by the majority ridiculous and mythical[;] nevertheless, to this transcriber spiritual communings are a fragment of, and as inherent as, life itself."[59] Becoming increasingly devout, he was baptized at St. Anthony's on March 8, 1952, at the age of fifty-five (there is no record of any earlier baptism for him, although records do exist for his siblings Olympia, Alfred, and Palmira), and on December 6 of that year he had his First Communion.

In a final attempt to share his spiritual experiences with others, Rizzoli began a new project on February 9, 1950, which he would work on for the rest of his life. This was the A.C.E., or AMTE's *Celestial Extravag(r)anza*,[60] a compilation of over three hundred and twenty-five 24 by 36-inch graphite on vellum sheets originally intended to poetically reproduce his "sunbursts" of visions linking poetry and architecture, but which he came to believe were the basis for the third, and final, testament of the Bible. A.M.T.E. (or Miss Amte, as he formally referred to her) was introduced to his readers in the first poem of the A.C.E., his personification of Architecture Made To Entertain,[61] a virginal consort of Christ who was Rizzoli's mentor, guide, and "principal collaborator."[62] She partnered him through the A.C.E.'s 2,600 pages[63] of poetry, prose, and graphic imagery as he attempted to reproduce the words and visions of saints, historic heroes, departed family members, and even Christ himself[64] through means "acceptable to spiritual authorities."[65]

Each sheet of the A.C.E. was equally divided into eight 8 1/2 by 11-inch sections, as if it were intended to be cut and bound to book size. Creating the A.C.E. "required the sacrifice of being in the mood," he commented, "a form of living with one foot on earth, the other in heaven, that is, stretching the imagination to the breaking point – a practice not recommended while payment of bills is

pending."[66] Rizzoli chose vellum as a medium due to its similarities to parchment – utilized by the ancient scribes – and because of its luminosity. Perhaps even more important for him was that use of vellum facilitated potential "mass production" and dissemination of his work through blueprinting processes. (This apparently took priority over his desire to use color, which was impossible in this medium, a loss he periodically lamented.)

Although he credited his mother as his inspiration in attempting poetry,[67] he emphasized that his work was directed by spiritual "collaborators." These included imaginary suppliants (those petitioning to transform the poem or image from his private vision into the transcribed reality of the "public domain"), serenaders, participants, witnesses, and others whom he felt contributed to or guided these visions. There were so many potential partners that "for easy reference" he selected those whose feast days coincided with the date of each vision.[68] All collaborators were credited as coauthors at the end of each poem; despite professional differences – as well as divergences across countries and centuries – they cooperated to bring each poem to its successful conclusion. Poem 879–3–x, for example, featured Michelangelo as the serenader, Saints Cyril and Methodius as suppliants, French sculptor Jules Dalou as a participant, Enrico Caruso witnessing, and Rechi Tacteur, a pseudonym for Miss Amte (an anagram for *architecture*), as the liaison between heaven and earth.

Apparently the church's roster of saints was insufficient for Rizzoli's needs, so he introduced new ones; his collaborators thus included bona fide saints as well as those that he anointed, including family members, venerated historical, political, and artistic figures, and in particular, both famous and unknown architects from preceding centuries. (Despite Rizzoli's professed disdain for anything other than Beaux-Arts architectural idioms, he joined Frank Lloyd Wright and Bernard Maybeck with such earlier luminaries as Christopher Wren and Andrea Palladio

WALLS DEL VERSE

POETRY UNTO STONE DONE

FRED CROSSDEGREE, *SPONSOR*
ABETTED FINANCIALLY BY HIS
SPOUSE AND THEIR DAUGHTER

"POETRY IS SO BEAUTIFUL THAT I'M LITERALLY
LIVING HEAD OVER HEELS WAY UP HIGH ABOVE
ITS EXHILARATING ATMOSPHERIC STATICS IN
SPITE OF OUR MANY EXCEEDINGLY INTRIGUING
VOCALLY SONOROUS BELLES." *CROSSDEGREE*

PROJECTED   MAJOR UNIT

SITE N° 11 IN THE

PIAFORE N° 22
PAR VALUE $30.00   DEC. 1937

COPANHAGEN
AND RIZZOLI
DELINEATORS

WALLS DEL VERSE. 1937. INK
ON RAG PAPER, 19¾ X 12"
(50.2 X 30.5 CM). COLLECTION
KENNETH W. K. LEUNG, NEW YORK

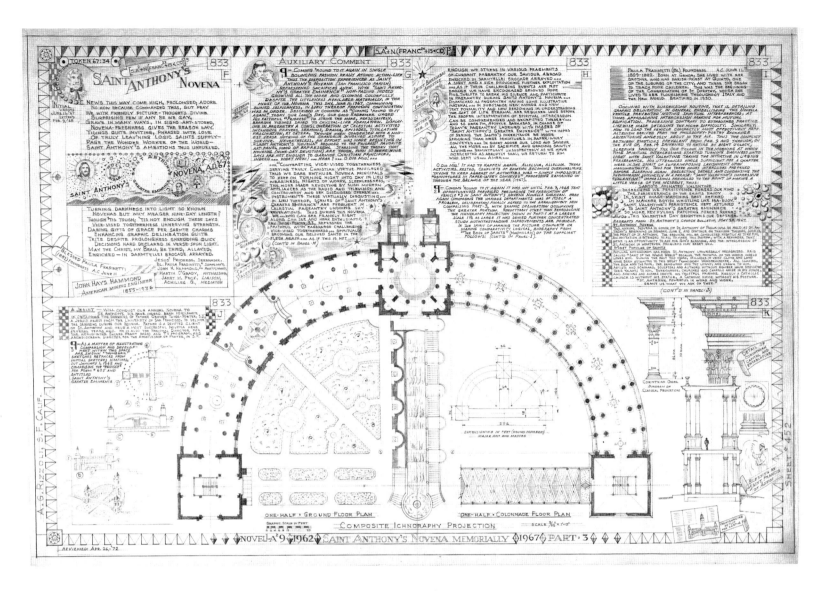

A.C.E. 452: NOVELLA #9 —
SAINT ANTHONY'S NOVENA
MEMORIALLY, PART 3. 1967.
GRAPHITE ON VELLUM, 24 X 36"
(61 X 91.4 CM). COLLECTION
THE AMES GALLERY, BERKELEY

to assist in his efforts.) Many collaborators were assigned new names or titles reflecting their new positions and responsibilities.[69]

Rizzoli initially developed his verses on whatever paper he had available, often the back of an envelope, usually "longhanding" at least two attempts before carefully lettering the refined poem onto the vellum. In the early years he composed and transcribed the poems on the same day; later it sometimes took many days, or even weeks or months before he would get around to formally recording his earlier compositions. He blamed "negligence" for his delay in formalizing his earlier sketches and verses; by 1966 he indicated that "awkwardness of living"[70] also interfered. "Pictorial composition . . . require[s] many hours of preliminary layout studies before final, painstaking detailing

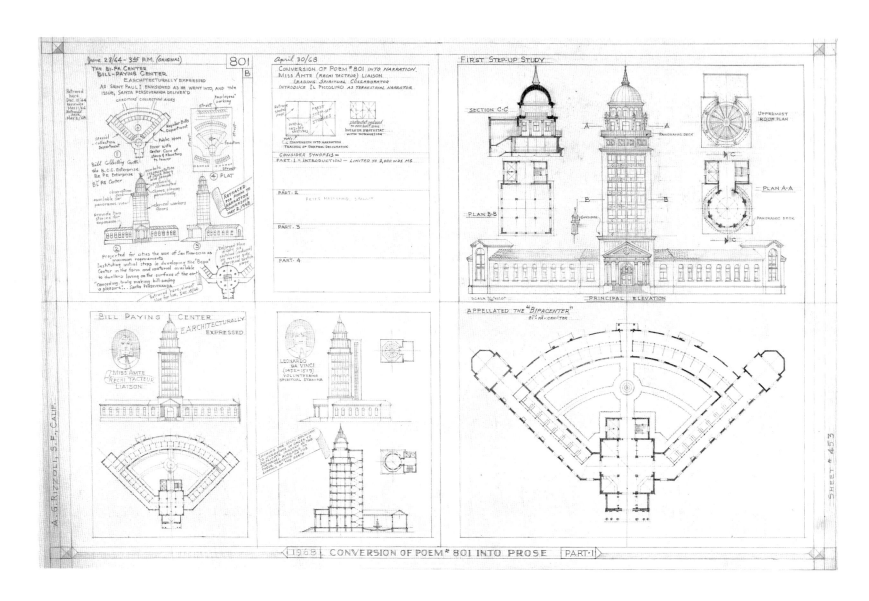

can be accomplished," he moaned. "All this, expected of one man to do, is simply outrageous."[71]

Rizzoli had considered typing his verses, but decided that "this reflected a method lacking artisticality." Alternatively, hand lettering enabled him to add "a variety of marginal embellishments" including "novelty sketches," biblical citations, and occasionally even short biographies of saints to complement and decorate the verses.[72] Later, when he began quoting "saintly intercessions" (i.e., dialogues with or directives from spiritual sources), the freedom allowed by hand lettering provided for greater ease in distinguishing the spiritual voices and accentuating them with illustrations of his accompanying visions.

The A.C.E. poems and drawings are frequently interrupted with lists of his accomplishments to date, inventorying the pages by the collaborators' names, dates, and "earthly careers"; by poetic rhythm; by poem title; by area of interest, and so on. The lists helped organize the material for the publishers he futilely solicited to accept his work;[73] after that failed, he included his own marketing pitches in the body of the text: "Like Candy, Keep it Handy," he exhorted.[74] There is no evidence to indicate that anything was ever sold.

He took his poetry very seriously, but felt that full communication of his message was limited by poetic constraints: "this transcriber [experienced] . . . severe agony while poring o'er what form of versification should be selected for transcription. This alone is a wearying ordeal; however, in doing God's will it must be endured."[75] His poem length was determined by practical considerations such as the number of stanzas he could print on his paper, and he was conservative about patterning and rhyming, maintaining strict self-imposed rules which determined how certain poetic devices could be applied. For example, ". . . departed male souls were allowed three 8-line stanzas, iambic pentameters, regular rhyming[, and] departed female souls [were] allowed 28 lines, closeknit stanza, iambic pentameters, couplet-rhyming."[76] Even his lettering was precisely determined: "Lettering slanting right depicting [Abraham] Lincoln serenading[,] and lettering slanting left, sainted spirits."[77] For all of Rizzoli's agonizing

over poetic conventions, however, the results were amateurish, with forced rhymes, pedantic rhythm, and often inscrutable subject matter. "Murmurs, baffling mumblings, buzzy-whisp'rings almost vocal-like at times," he moaned, "do . . . literary chaos make when whittled down to meet meter requirements."[78]

Rizzoli acquired no greater poetic expertise over the years. At times, the titles of his verses indicated a theme that was developed only tangentially in the body of the poem; other times, there seemed to be no connection at all. Many titles were extremely cryptic, utilizing invented words that may or may not have been defined in the text; others – primarily single word titles – appeared to have been selected for their placement in an alphabetical line-up rather than for any reason of content. And throughout, Rizzoli mingled events and circumstances of daily life with his private, spiritual experiences, making it a challenge to discern which is which.

The first part of the A.C.E. is composed solely of poetry. Rizzoli's auxiliary comments make clear that he forced himself to work in this medium, that he struggled with it, and that he was consistently tempted to express his visions graphically rather than verbally. As he continued to work, he came to realize that both media could function together; consequently, later pages include increasing numbers of architectural illustrations complementing the poems. These varied in complexity between simple sketches and more elaborate drawings including elevations, details of facade treatments, and, on rare occasion, furnishings or internal mechanical elements.[79] Apparently, he never really became reconciled to the integration of the two genres, however, for he discussed and lamented the conflict between drawing and writing throughout the A.C.E., and changed his emphasis on one or the other almost daily; the resulting combination of the two on many pages recalls illuminated medieval manuscripts.[80]

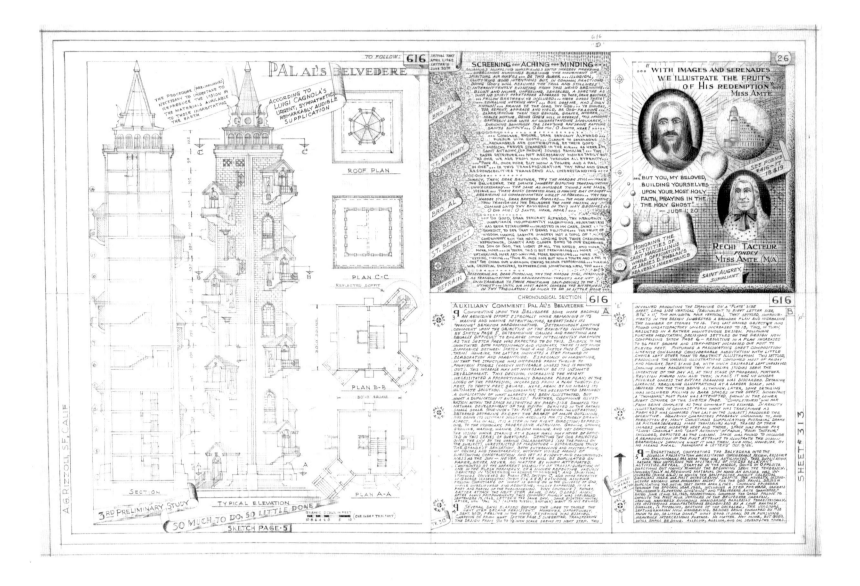

Rizzoli emphasized his role as author throughout the A.C.E. by recording his name (in one form or title or another) on almost every section of every page.[81] The different labels he used included his alter ego Il Piccolino (also Little One or Littl'Un), and a variety of titles such as Transcriber, Translator, Delineator, Curator, Organizer, Promoter, and even stranger appellations such as Jelly Maker, Zitherist, and Embalmer.[82] By repeatedly calling attention to himself he underscored that he anticipated readers for his opus; indeed, he welcomed an audience for this work, much as he had attempted to attract one by self-publishing his novel or advertising the A.T.E. exhibits in earlier years: ". . . wishing others would share this marvelous wandering into the wonders giving form to Heaven's

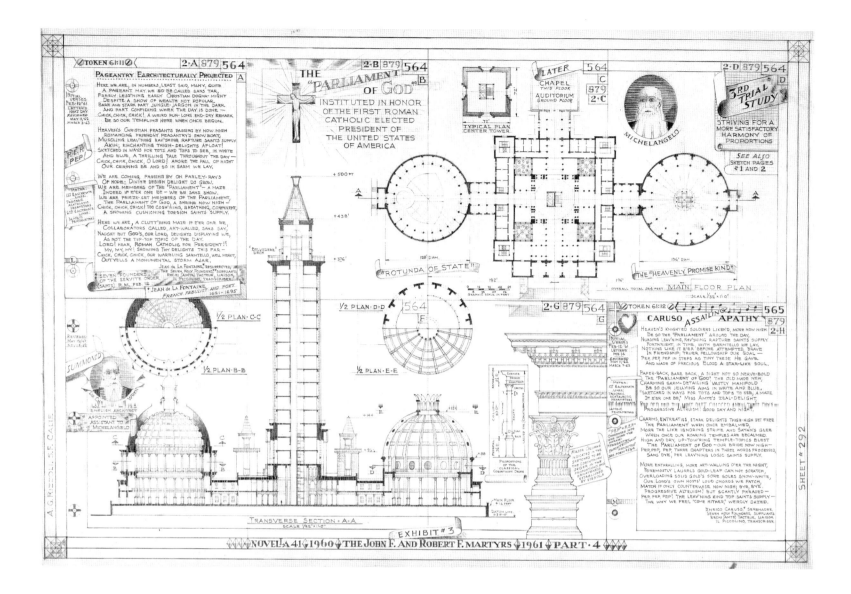

many mysterifying categories, . . .[83] regrettably, to date, without success."[84] He later admitted "at long last realizing an opus of this nature has a limited follow[ing], almost nil . . . ,"[85] yet felt that although "the terrestrial audience may venture ridicule; on the other hand, the celestial audience simply cannot feel but otherwise."[86]

Given his profound Roman Catholic beliefs, it is not surprising that Rizzoli found "no need to scrape round nor roam" for source material for his poems, for the "saints supply designs, clues, splays, zeal, music, sculpture, art."[87] Rizzoli's initial sonnets addressed the theme of "Uncovering the Poetry in Architecture"[88] through subjects as diverse as different architectural styles (including log cabins, Swiss chalets, castles, chateaux, shanties, and palaces);

A.C.E. 292: NOVELLA 41 — THE JOHN F. AND ROBERT F. MARTYRS, PART 4. 1961. GRAPHITE ON VELLUM, 24 X 36" (61 X 91.4 CM). COLLECTION THE AMES GALLERY, BERKELEY

words of interest to him, arranged alphabetically (poems to Adventure, Basilica, and so on); secular holidays (New Year's Day, Mother's Day, and Labor Day, among others); patriotic holidays or events (such as the Presidents' birthdays in February, Memorial Day, Independence Day, and California's Admission Day); and Catholic holidays or events (St. Patrick's Day, changes in the papacy, Easter, Saints' Days, priesthood anniversaries for Church elders, and so on). Occasionally unusual topics would be included, such as an unexpected snowfall in San Francisco (Poem 610); hair, since he felt he was "thinning out on top" (Poem 874); the game of chess (Poems 746, 747, 765, 778);[89] finding an old jar of home canned peaches put up by his mother some twenty years earlier (Poem 197); leap year, which he liked (Poem 776); or daylight saving time, which he didn't (Poems 359–60). Although he started his opus with the intended theme of revealing the poetry in architecture, ultimately he included a much greater range of subject matter than he had initially conceived.[90]

Almost seven years after he began the A.C.E., the heavenly "assistant" (in this case, John F. Kennedy) for the first time matter-of-factly noted that this document formed the third testament of the Bible.[91] Subsequently this became the stated raison d'être for Rizzoli's efforts, his interpretation of the celestial source of his visions, and explanation of his role as transcriber. The subject matter of the later poems became darker, and the religious apparitions more pronounced, as he became more preoccupied with death, concentrating on eulogizing the departed – from his mother, brother, and sister to President Kennedy to the local archbishop – through the creation of architectural edifices dedicated to them. Many of Rizzoli's final poems, prose "auxiliary comments," and architectural sketches commemorated people that he knew only in passing, such as members of his church; these often included obituaries copied in full from the local newspaper, since he knew nothing else about them.

Rizzoli evinced little personal interest in producing these works, but felt he was required by God to do so: "merely looking at the latest [vision] . . . brought on mental agony bearing witness to heed God's will or suffer the consequences . . . ."[92]

Because of their more relaxed approach, the prose commentaries he somewhat sheepishly appended to his verses ("If it is poetry there's no need of walking on crutches"[93]) possess a more internalized rhythm, due in part to a rather lyrical use of alliteration, stylized words, and phrasing. Despite his complex, grandiose, and idiosyncratic syntax and vocabulary, undisciplined compulsion to create, and *horror vacuui*, Rizzoli's prose is often expressive and moving. The commentaries functioned as diary, confessional, and newsletter as much as clarification and elaboration of the poems.

The saintly intercessions are most commonly included in these prose portions of the A.C.E.; their physical layout, the stylized wording used to introduce, reveal, and close them, and their altered lettering style and graphics are repeated with little variation throughout. These effects underscore the special significance of these sections; based on Freud's theories of the "repetition compulsion," some psychiatrists would claim that through such reiteration Rizzoli attempted to control the circumstances of these visions,[94] although they do not appear to diminish either in intensity or quantity over time. In his case it may be more appropriate to suggest that the repetition of these effects is evocative of the experience of prayer.

Rizzoli defended his visions by reminding his readers that people were aware of light, sound, and electrical waves, so perhaps spiritual waves had simply not yet been scientifically discovered and charted. These waves, he believed, floated in the atmosphere, bridging generations, and were the source for all creative ideas, including his own.[95] Rizzoli specifically attributed his creativity to his asceticism and openness to God, and belittled those who credited their own intellect as the source of their inspirations. He hypothesized that intelligence could be acquired from the "inheritances" of souls of previous generations, but wished for a simple algebraic formula "similar to

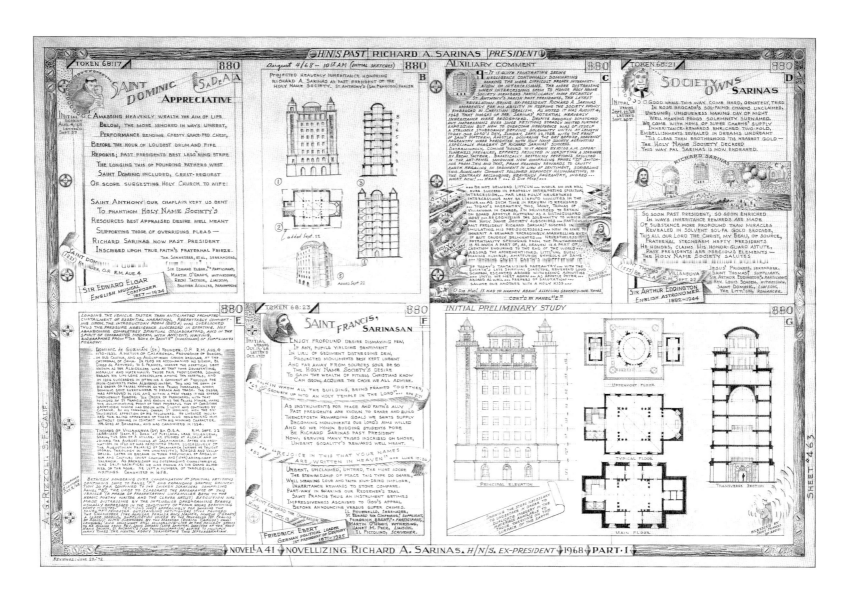

A.C.E. 463: Novella 41 —
Novellizing Richard A.
Sarinas, H.N.S. Ex-President,
Part 1. 1968. Graphite
on vellum, 24 x 36" (61 x
91.4 cm). Collection The
Ames Gallery, Berkeley

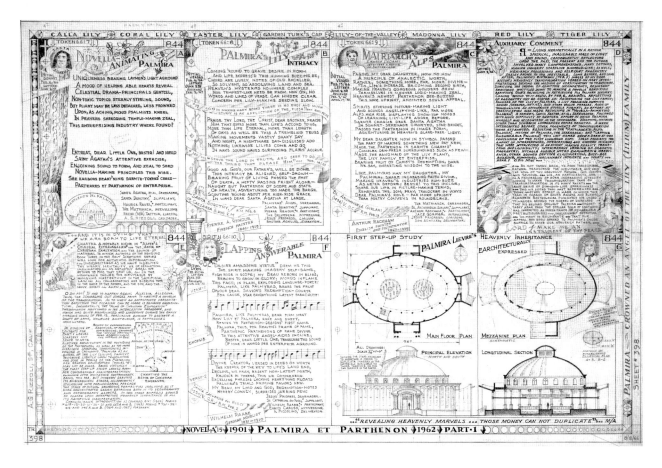

A=B/C=D=What?"[96] to describe the origin of creativity, so that it might be more easily comprehended (and, one suspects, mathematically proven). In Rizzoli's hypothetical equation, A=the Almighty, B=the Bible, C=Christ, and D=Decorative Architecture;[97] thus did he again intrinsically link architecture with spiritualism and religious belief.

Through their intercessions, the saints and spiritual guides coached him, supported him, and inspired him, attempting to reassure him by explaining their purpose and his responsibilities. They also occasionally threatened, however, urging him to "continue diligently to the end,"[98] reminding him that it was their understanding that he was being kept alive solely for the purpose of transcribing the visions they provided him.[99] His designs occasionally elicited specific disapproval from the more critical heavenly professionals, as, for example, when architects François Mansard and Antonio Sangallo indicated that the aesthetics of Rizzoli's projects needed improvement,[100] and later referred to his work as "at best vague . . . and amateurish . . . ."[101] How much greater a sting did this criticism have coming from his heavenly mentors rather than from his own self-critical musings!

The illustrations accompanying the intercessions are markedly different from Rizzoli's other drawings: they are sketchier, more gestural, drawn with a faster and more agitated motion, and typically include representations of natural phenomena such as lightning bolts, stars, spatial debris, explosions, meteors, and so on, hinting at the agitation of these visionary experiences. Later intercessionary graphics included sketches of angels, praying figures, and other figurative references, as well as evocative exclamations. "Ridiculing, raving, riding, rocketing, roar, roar, away, O Lord! What? What are we hearing?" he questioned himself, before calmly answering, "Nothing new, simply mental disturbances, likening brain cells bursting, that's all."[102]

He endlessly described his increasing difficulties and how he created under great pressure, responding with artistic expression in an instinctual attempt to obtain relief from his agitation. His manner of working recalls that of Wölfli's:

When he creates, it is in a state at once sublime and oppressed, ruled by a powerful inner tension, by something concrete, serious, and measured, yet fully personal, violent, and turned toward the absolute. It is both supreme freedom and the most painful torture.[103]

Yet unlike most other artists who work at this intensity of passion and pain, Rizzoli was able to candidly yet calmly describe his agony, carefully dating and documenting each visionary experience over a period of decades:

Confusion, inability to mobilize the mechanics of recording impressions automatically, for the most part dwelling in a sphere of shifting sand-like maze of color, paste, light and sound . . . .[104]

The effort of creating new poems and illustrations became more and more difficult as he aged; "'pictures' in the head and behavior of hand often do not cooperate," he complained.[105] Rizzoli became increasingly agitated about his inability to graphically reproduce what he saw in "the eye of the mind, its shape and magnitude and color forever changing"[106] in "a supernatural perpetual display."[107] This was the source of much of Rizzoli's agitation, for in contrast to artists such as Wölfli for whom the process of creation was apparently more important than the outcome,[108] Rizzoli's goal was the accurate reproduction of his visions, and his inability to accomplish this caused him great anguish.[109] The incongruence between vision and transcription was particularly problematic due to his belief that his images were not the product of his own intellect or creativity, but the result of specific prompting from celestial sources. The A.C.E. prose commentary is annotated with myriad notes lamenting that his creative efforts lacked the splendor of his visions, hampered as they were by such logistical constraints as paper size, the time required to record them by hand, conflicts with his other responsibilities, his lack of "scholastical degrees,"[110] and his own drafting inadequacies. He nevertheless kept working, with passion but increasingly little pleasure, to bring his visions out into the "public domain."

Most years he created a poem or poems, often with auxiliary comment, at the time of his own birthday, for, sadly, he expected to receive "greeting from heavenly dwellers only."[111] Some years he also received "heavenly gifts"; for his sixty-fifth birthday in 1961 there was the "Beamingbellabay," a heavenly architectural edifice dedicated to him; he received "La Fane Haspine" in 1962 and the "Tokenquay" in 1963. Although pleased with these "God-Animated" gifts, he lamented his increasing years; musing on his seventy-sixth birthday in 1972, he condensed spiritual congratulations into "one simple line: 'Remember Thou Too Die Must.' Quite contrary to traditional birthday greetings!"[112]

As he aged, Rizzoli increasingly complained about losing track of time: of hours turned into minutes, months into days, as he lost touch with reality and became immersed to an ever greater extent in his private visions. "O Fleeting Time!" he cried, "Why thy cyclonic speed?"[113] When he was unable to transfer them to paper, the images, verses, or "other contingencies, such as monumentality, ornateness, structural stability, type of materials, illumination, importance, relevant function, et cetera" were left "drifting aimlessly about in the sky."[114] "Visions visions, visions!" he exclaimed. "First appearing as icebergs, slowly melting into water and then into their permanent gaseous state . . . to their heavenly origin. . . ."[115]

His decreasing energy led him to recopy earlier verses and images, sometimes with revisions or additions, sometimes as originally composed or with minor changes in proportion or detail. It also led him to redesign his page format into his so-called Novella form.[116] Nevertheless, aside from this repetition and a somewhat formulaic approach to calendrical events (which was consistent throughout the A.C.E.), there was no significant conceptual or physical

degradation in Rizzoli's works as he aged. The structural composition of his architectural designs continued in the same eclectic vein, and his prose and poetry continued to be dense, elaborate, and compulsive. The last A.C.E. works include fewer narrated spiritual intercessions; those that do appear reveal even greater agony and agitation: "Indeed, what now! Hear? . . . Bugs darkening sky birds are falling rats squealing cats meowing dogs barking wolves howling . . . herds stampeding buffaloes rolling rolling . . . O Dio Mio! . . ."[117]

Work on the A.C.E. continued until February 23, 1977. With his last vellum (titled "Rest in Peace . . Awhile") uncompleted, Rizzoli suffered a stroke as he was walking down the street. Curiously, he was found in an area rather far from his home, and it took some time for the police to identify him and locate any kin. His niece and her family cleared out the house after his stroke, although it remained vacant for a while in the interim and may have been subject to some theft during that time. The proceeds from the sale of the house were used to support Rizzoli during the last four years of his life in a convalescent home in Santa Rosa. Members of the family, who lived nearby, visited him periodically, but Rizzoli never regained the power of speech or movement. He died on November 18, 1981, at the age of eighty-five, and the family conscientiously implemented his plans for his funeral, which he had specifically outlined and paid for years in advance. Rizzoli is buried next to his mother in a cemetery near San Francisco.

Through his drawings and writings, A. G. Rizzoli escaped his reality as the low-paid blue-collar son of poor immigrants, becoming a collaborator with God, protégé of the saints, and companion to heroic figures from past and present. Shame at his family's dysfunction, guilt from his repressed sexual feelings, and self-denigration for his ascetic, friendless existence were mitigated by the enhanced self-esteem he developed through his creations. Unable to achieve his ambition to create architectural works for others, he created them for himself. His work helped him to reorder and balance his existence and restored his sense of personal worth: it reduced his feeling of alienation from the real world and brought him a new measure of both protection and control. Periodically using the metaphor of the ship, with a "cargo" of poems and drawings, he sought salvation and satisfaction through his spiritual voyage. Again and again, amazed by his own output, he sought to uncover the origin of creativity; his deep religious beliefs always provided a sufficient explanation, however, and he did not look for sources beyond those that he interpreted as heaven-sent.

The rich iconography of Rizzoli's drawings is tempered with self-consciousness and self-aggrandizement as he reminds us that *he* was the one chosen to transcribe these heavenly visions. He described himself as the "High Prince," the "First degree, Master Architect and Master Builder" and his work as "the most magnificent . . . neo-architecture mankind can ever hope to see."[118] But his pride in his work alternated with intense feelings of incompetence as he regularly fell short of his personal ideals in recording the spiritual imagery and verses that he beheld.

Rizzoli's determination to share his creations with others resulted from his feeling that dissemination of his works would benefit humankind: "No . . . longer any reason for feeling lonely," he proclaimed on the front of the *A.T.E. Portfolio*. He believed that his works, a gift to him from spiritual sources, should in turn be passed on to others, and he anticipated that they would inspire a devotional response, mitigating others' alienation as they did his own. "Every line has a meaning all its own," he wrote. "Verily marble dust we gather and use, each particle . . . firmly cemented together with the spirit of cooperation immersed in the sweetest passion of all, the love of giving."[119]

Although he craved public acknowledgment and commendation, his work paradoxically isolated him even further, as his immersion in it drew him further away from reality with the creation of a second identity that could not be shared. Although his drawings superficially presented public spaces, in reality they depicted private, symbolic sanctuaries. He used historical idioms to dignify

A.T.E. PORTFOLIO — COVER.
DIAZO PRINT ON PAPER,
34 x 18" (86.4 x 45.7 CM).
COLLECTION THE AMES GALLERY,
BERKELEY

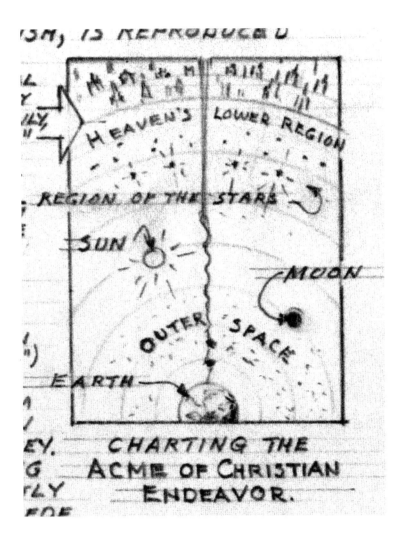

and validate his work, but there is no evidence that Rizzoli ever really expected that his projects would be executed, although apparently they *could* have been: there are no records of any discussions or correspondence with engineers, developers, or others who might have transposed his work into three dimensions. No drawings for structural elements or decorative interiors exist, and the rare landscaping he depicted was stylized and almost surreal, in keeping with the aesthetic of his architecture, but unwelcoming for the public. The enigmatic language barriers of his encoded invented vocabulary also impeded full communication of his message. It seems unlikely, therefore, that his buildings were intended for human habitation; rather, Rizzoli seemed content to have them function as works on paper, their main intent being artistic, symbolic, and religious.

Simultaneously living in two worlds, spending his days in one reality, his nights and weekends in another, each with a separate identity, Rizzoli was apparently successful in maintaining a sense of objectivity about this contradiction, as well as an ability to distinguish between the two. "With one foot on the earth and the other in heaven, the entire universe is easily observable; this distortion is physical . . . more than mental . . . ," he wrote.[120] It is clear that his role as "earthly architectural assistant and transcriber" to God held greater interest – and, in a sense, reality – for him. It was a world to which he felt he was more properly suited, a world with grand buildings, poetry, stellar masters of art and literature, morality, and culture. His utopia did not exist in a vacuum, however; it derived from and was stimulated by the external world, for his work references people he knew, holidays he celebrated, deaths he mourned. While his work reveals a significant degree of personal dysfunction, it concurrently exhibits a tremendous amount of control, coherence, and even logic. His labors were authentic and purposeful, creating a valuable structure that he believed reduced his internal agitation and enabled him to creatively address, if not master, his mental turmoil and agony.

Rizzoli's personal isolation and internal torments were not the cause of his art, but conditions that helped to determine the parameters within which he worked. Free of academic conventions and social restraints yet not ignorant of them, aware of the outside world yet separated from it through a self-imposed solitude, his work developed gradually as his visions of utopia evolved into a true alternate reality – anarchistic and unobtainable yet deliberate, powerful, and expressive. No single crisis appears to have precipitated his labors, but the attachment to his mother, the trauma of his father's disappearance and death, and his sexual frustrations all impacted both his work and his life. Since the announcement of his oeuvre, art and architectural historians, psychiatrists, and theologians have debated his symptoms and expressions in a perhaps misguided attempt to diagnose his mental condition. Although he appears to have displayed some of the traits common to certain psychopathological conditions,[121] he was both more objective and coherent in his creative expressions than is typical of those suffering from such disorders. Further, his punning and playful wit underscore a clear degree of control over his material, as his ability to hold a full-time job reveals control in terms of his daily routine.

Rizzoli's work thus challenges the conceptual and somewhat arbitrary borders that end-of-the-millennium theorists have constructed between imagination and insanity, as it concurrently challenges our aesthetic and cultural norms. Masterfully expressing both his vulnerability and a sense of personal power, his work is at once passive and assertive, urgent and lyrical, Edenic and absurd. It is humorous and pathetic, evocative and mysterious.

Whatever may ultimately be determined about the man, Rizzoli's "labors" will stand as a phenomenal achievement. Raw strength of vision and purpose articulated through meticulous craftsmanship, personal faith offered up as public structure, A. G. Rizzoli has finally found his audience.

ACHILLES G. RIZZOLI. 1918.
GELATIN SILVER PRINT.
3⅞ X 2⁹⁄₁₆" (9.9 X 6.5 CM).
PHOTOGRAPHER UNKNOWN.
COLLECTION THE ESTATE OF
THE ARTIST

THE
JOY
(A BIT OF HEAVENLY ARCHITECTURE)
ZONE

BY JOHN BEARDSLEY

1915. It was the worst and the best of years for nineteen-year-old Achilles G. Rizzoli. It was the year his father borrowed a shotgun, disappeared into the Marin County hills, and blasted himself into eternity. It was also the year of the Panama-Pacific International Exposition, an architectural confection with utopian aspirations that rose and fell in a matter of months on the edge of the San Francisco Bay. The two events bore no outward connection to each other, but both would convulse Rizzoli's life – the one a nightmare that shadowed his existence for years to come; the other a vision of a more perfect dominion that impelled his architectural investigations for at least as long. The two may even have become linked in Rizzoli's mind, as if one defined the antithesis of the other. The Panama-Pacific Exposition was Rizzoli's first compelling experience with the romantic and inspirational aspects of neoclassical architecture and provided him with a point of departure in the unfolding of his own visionary designs. There are pronounced similarities between the exposition and Rizzoli's own utopian dream, Y.T.T.E., meaning Yield To Total Elation. And there are parallels between the eclectic forms of its architecture and the fabulous concoction of styles Rizzoli deployed when portraying his family, friends, and acquaintances as buildings. But the exposition seems to have answered emotional as well as artistic needs. There are hints in Rizzoli's work that his fantastical schemes and his symbolic portraits were a projection of the feelings of loss and longing that were a fixture of his life in this world.

Rizzoli was no stranger to architectural conventions before the Panama-Pacific Exposition. He spent four years at the Oakland Polytechnic College of Engineering, where he studied architectural drafting along with mechanics, electricity, magnetism, and civil architecture. When he left the school in 1915, he demonstrated his capabilities by drawing *City Hall,* a perfectly workmanlike rendering of a neoclassical domed structure with colonnaded porticoes. Nor would that be the end of his training. From 1916 to 1923, he was a member of the San Francisco Architectural Club, established to promote "serious and systematic architectural study among the younger men of the profession." In practice, it was primarily a proving ground for draftsmen who couldn't afford the time or the expense of attending architectural school full time. (Rizzoli himself was working in these years, first as a draftsman at Hicks Iron Works, then for architect John Foley.) The club offered lectures, studios, and critiques by recognized local architects with the aim of improving both rendering and design skills. There is no documentation of Rizzoli's participation in club activities, but any involvement would have deepened his familiarity with academic neoclassicism of his technical education.

Rizzoli's training suggests an exposure to the principles of architectural drafting and design based on the conventions of the Ecole des Beaux-Arts in Paris, which set the standard for architectural education in America in the early decades of the twentieth century. This exposure is confirmed by Gerry Holt, who was a colleague of Rizzoli's between 1939 and 1941 at the firm of Otto Deichmann, where Rizzoli was employed as a draftsman from the mid-1930s until 1970. Holt says Rizzoli "grew up in the Beaux-Arts," especially through his experience at the Architectural Club, which he says "was seriously inclined in those days."[1] Beaux-Arts–inspired instruction would have furnished Rizzoli with a wide repertory of forms based on historical precedent, drawn primarily from antiquity and the Renaissance but encompassing Gothic and Romanesque as well. It would also have given him an exposure to compositional principles stressing unity and order achieved through axial and radial plans, the symmetrical disposition of forms, the proportions of the classical orders, and harmonious decorative schemes. Just as important, the Beaux-Arts tradition of the *projet rendu,* or presentation drawing, would have provided Rizzoli with methods and standards for rendering, which he would exploit with growing authority and expressiveness over the years.

Beaux-Arts presentation drawings generally depicted hypothetical building projects, intended to demonstrate the student's understanding of architectural ideas and forms. They were based on *esquisses* (sketches), to which they had to correspond in all essentials. Final drawings were executed in ink and ink wash over pencil, and were often large (up to a meter in length), highly detailed, and very time-consuming to produce, sometimes requiring as much as two or three months. The exacting standards to which they had to conform were an expression of their importance in architectural education – they were submitted for judging in monthly competitions (*concours d'émulation*) that determined a student's advancement. Often, several drawings were presented at the *concours,*

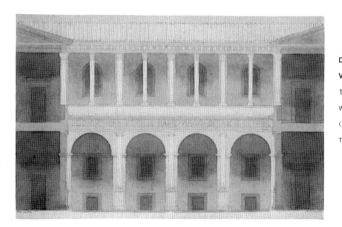

DEO-CPT-MAX-ET-DIVE-MARIE-VIRGINI-GLORIOSE-DEI-PARE. 1912. GRAPHITE AND INK WASH ON PAPER, 11 X 16¹⁵⁄₁₆" (27.9 X 43 CM). COLLECTION THE ESTATE OF THE ARTIST

showing plans, elevations, sections, and details of the decorative schemes. Generally, elevations showed the principal facade and were presented without reference to an urban or landscape context. They were also depicted without benefit of perspective; instead, shadows were used to indicate depth.[2]

At the higher levels of study, and especially for the *Grand Prix de Rome* – the annual prize that conferred on the winner the opportunity to study at public expense for several years in Rome – competition programs called for the design of some kind of civil or ecclesiastical megastructure, which could be a palace or cathedral, public bath, school, library, hospital, monument, or cenotaph. (Rarely were commercial or industrial projects included in the programs.) Over the years, these hypothetical structures became so elaborate and the renderings so bombastic that the resulting images took on a life quite apart from any actualities they purported to describe. They became *objets d'art*, something tacitly acknowledged in the annual public exhibitions held in conjunction with the judging for the *Grand Prix de Rome*. Jury deliberations themselves were private – not even the students were present. This would change in American architectural schools, in an effort to make critiques part of the learning experience.[3]

In his symbolic portraits and in his elevations of buildings for y.t.t.e., Rizzoli demonstrated a familiarity with the conventions of Beaux-Arts rendering. Both the large scale of his drawings and the means of execution were consistent with the Beaux-Arts model, as was the representation of the principal elevation without the use of perspective and without reference to any meaningful context. Rizzoli likewise used shadow to great effect in representing depth, along with color washes in graduated tones. The vast repertory of architectural styles in his drawings confirms the Beaux-Arts predilection for the free combination of historical prototypes, while the bravado of his structures recalls the hyperbole of Beaux-Arts programs, at least at the higher levels of competition. Beginning in August 1935 and continuing annually for the next five to six years, Rizzoli hosted an open house on the first Sunday of the month to show his drawings, which he called the Achilles Tectonic Exhibit (a.t.e.). This may have been intended to mimic the annual exhibition of *Prix de Rome* renderings. Even the wry evaluations that Rizzoli appended to his drawings, in which he graded his own abilities and those of his supposed collaborators, expressed his understanding of the significance of these renderings as proof of a draftsman's general competence.

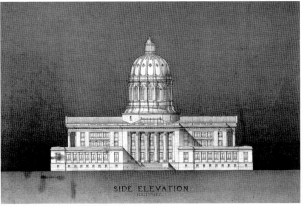

CITY HALL. 1915. INK ON RAG PAPER, 17½ X 23¹¹⁄₁₆" (44.5 X 60.2 CM). COLLECTION THE AMES GALLERY, BERKELEY

CITY HALL. 1915. INK ON RAG PAPER, 17⁵⁄₁₆ X 24⁵⁄₁₆" (44 X 62.4 CM). COLLECTION THE AMES GALLERY, BERKELEY

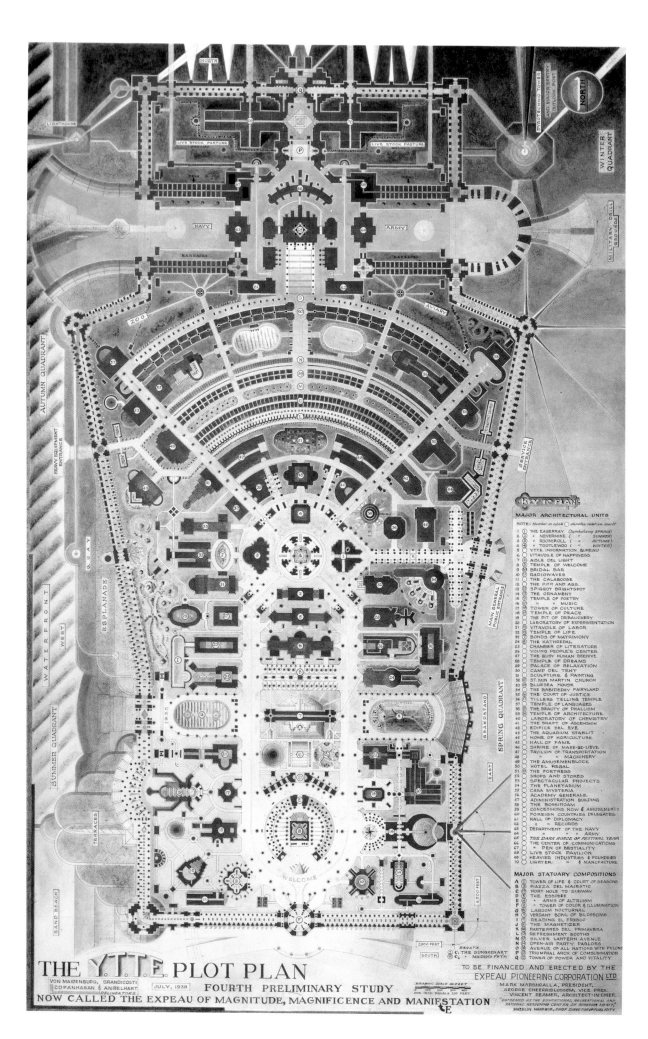

THE Y.T.T.E. PLOT PLAN —
FOURTH PRELIMINARY STUDY.
1938. INK ON RAG PAPER,
38¼ x 24¼" (97.2 x 61.6 CM).
COLLECTION THE AMES GALLERY,
BERKELEY

While his drawings show strong similarities to their Beaux-Arts model, Rizzoli was clearly no slave to convention. He presented plans, sections, and elevations along with significant ornamental details, but he frequently condensed these into a single drawing. He often sacrificed coherence and symmetry to attain greater expressiveness and character in his designs. And he incorporated lengthy texts, which is not consistent with Beaux-Arts rendering. He may have found a precedent for this in contemporaneous architectural textbooks, such as Banister Fletcher's *History of Architecture: On the Comparative Method* (first published in 1896). This book, which Rizzoli recommends reading in a 1940 portfolio of drawings for the A.T.E. "to appreciate fully the meaning of architecture," contains heavily annotated drawings of architectural details.[4]

Indeed, if Rizzoli had merely been a virtuoso draftsman in the Beaux-Arts tradition, he would not lay such a commanding claim on our attention. Rizzoli's work is well beyond the ordinary. It is over the top – wildly imaginative and amusing, full of visual and verbal puns and incongruous architectural juxtapositions. In later years, Rizzoli collected his projects under the acronym A.M.T.E., meaning Architecture Made to Entertain, which it certainly does. Beneath the surface, however, his work is also very poignant. Rizzoli was a visionary who saw architecture as an agent of personal and social transformation. It was an expression of his utopian longings and his desire for closer personal attachments (not to mention his sexual anxieties). Gerry Holt remembers him as "a quiet, mild-mannered, very kind and polite man, who never talked about his work." But it was his salvation from a solitary life, particularly after the death of his beloved mother in 1937. The cover of Rizzoli's 1940 exhibition portfolio, "featuring in particular the Y.T.T.E.," proclaims (with repetition presumably for added emphasis), "Now there's no more any longer any reason to feel lonely." In the same portfolio, he gives the text of the Y.T.T.E. theme song: "No More Alone."

Rizzoli used his knowledge of the conventions of Beaux-Arts rendering and the traditions of neoclassical architecture, to push them in fantastical ways – ways that were evidently revealed to him by the San Francisco Panama-Pacific Exposition. The exposition would have been Rizzoli's most forceful introduction to the social ambitions and the fanciful eclecticism of neoclassical architecture. Built on a 635-acre site in what is now the Marina district of San Francisco and intended to commemorate the

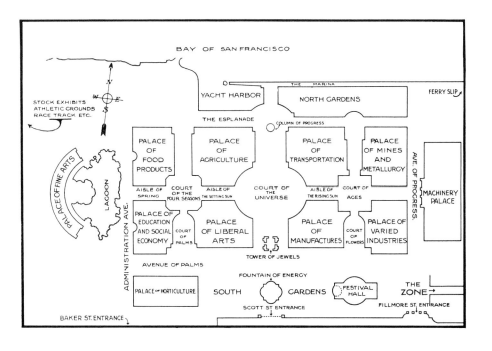

GROUND PLAN OF THE 1915 SAN FRANCISCO PANAMA-PACIFIC INTERNATIONAL EXPOSITION. REPRINTED IN PALACES AND COURTS OF THE EXPOSITION (SAN FRANCISCO, 1915), AS REPRODUCED IN BURTON BENEDICT, THE ANTHROPOLOGY OF WORLD'S FAIRS (BERKELEY: SCOLAR PRESS, 1983), 96. PHOTOGRAPHER UNKNOWN

opening of the Panama Canal, the exposition was also a paean to technological progress and to the rebirth of San Francisco from the ashes of the 1906 earthquake and fire. The exposition displayed the integration of the arts characteristic of Beaux-Arts design, with a rationalized plan, coordinated architectural styles, and a unified program of sculptural embellishment. Organized around spaces with grandiose names like the Court of the Universe, the Court of the Ages, and the Court of the Four Seasons, it featured eight major exhibition "palaces" clad in artificial travertine and devoted to themes such as agriculture, transportation, manufacturing, and liberal arts. For the most part, architects were given courts rather than buildings to create; the firm of McKim, Mead and White designed the Court of the Universe, Louis Christian Mullgardt the Court of the Ages, and Henry Bacon the Court of the Four Seasons. An exception was the Palace of Fine Arts, designed by Bernard Maybeck, which stood across a lagoon from the other exhibition halls; its principal facade featured an imposing curved colonnade half

surrounding a rotunda that seemed to hover over the waters of the lagoon. This proved to be one of the most popular buildings at the fair. It was also the only one that was spared from demolition, and is today the Exploratorium.

The Panama-Pacific Exposition confirmed how eclectic Beaux-Arts–inspired architecture had become, combining Greek and Roman, Romanesque and Renaissance, Moorish and Middle Eastern influences. John D. Barry's 1915 book *The City of Domes* (subtitled *A Walk with an Architect About the Courts and Palaces of the Panama-Pacific International Exposition*) describes the Court of the Universe as inspired by Bernini's entrance to St. Peter's Church in Rome. Barry also says the Palace of Horticulture was derived from the mosque of Ahmed the First in Constantinople and suggests that the rotunda of the Palace of Fine Arts was designed to evoke a Greek or Roman ruin. (Specifically, it may have been inspired by Piranesi's engraving of the ruins of the so-called Temple of Minerva Medica, from his 1764 *Views of Rome*.[5]) As if to underscore this romantic eclecticism, the exposition was peppered with exotic and spectacular effects. It featured a coordinated color scheme by the painter Jules Guerin based on the pastel hues of the California landscape. Pale shades of green, gold, ocher, and orange tinted columns, domes, and walls, evoking evergreen shrubs, tawny grass, brown hills, and fields of poppies. At night, magnesium lamps illuminated the palaces, while a special installation of forty-eight searchlights called the Scintillator raked the sky with artificial auroras. Red- and green-colored lights illuminated fountains and clouds of steam; the green glass dome of the Palace of Horticulture glowed from within, creating the impression of a gigantic opal. Most spectacular was the Tower of Jewels, at 432 feet the tallest feature of the exposition. Embellished with over 100,000 cut glass gems hung from wires and backed with mirrors, it sparkled in the breeze both day and night.[6]

While the fair was meant to dazzle, it was also intended to stimulate educational, cultural, and moral improvement in its visitors. Murals and sculptures provided allegorical representations of creativity, progress, and the genius of machinery, which guidebooks helped visitors decode. In a larger sense, the fair's unified plan and architectural design were themselves meant to be inspirational. Like the 1893 World's Columbian Exposition in Chicago on which it was patterned, the Panama-Pacific Exposition was an expression of the social ambitions of the City Beautiful Movement. A cultural, environmental, aesthetic, and political crusade with roots in civic improvement and urban park projects of the middle nineteenth century, the City Beautiful Movement sought to control and enhance the physical growth of cities through a combination of neoclassical architecture, formal plazas, and naturalistic landscape design. Though it would later be criticized for reliance on retrograde architectural styles and costly decorative schemes, it left a legacy of public buildings and monuments characterized by fine workmanship and detailing, along with systems of spacious parks, radial streets, and boulevards that are still, in some places at least, the best features of their urban environments.

But the ambitions of the movement went beyond urban improvement. City Beautiful architects and theorists such as Daniel Burnham, Warren Manning, and Charles Mulford Robinson believed that a salutary environment could influence both the hearts and the minds of the populace, leading to better citizens, more productive workers, and a better economic climate. Burnham pleaded for the development of architecturally coherent civic centers to replace the jumble of existing buildings, which "sadly disturbs our peacefulness and destroys that repose within us which is the true basis of all contentment." Robinson said such a civic center would be a "majestic thing and one better worth the devotion and service of its citizens," while J. G. Phelps Stokes believed that "The wider the public enjoyment of the beautiful features of a city, and the larger the numbers of people who enjoy those beauties together, the wider the mutual thoughts and feelings and interests . . . and this tends to the development of a wider social morality."[7] Significantly, the civic center envisioned by City Beautiful planners was deemed to be incompatible with commerce, which was relegated to a different sector.[8]

The rhetoric of moral, intellectual, and social improvement was emphatically part of the Panama-Pacific Exposition. The introduction to a 1915 guidebook, Benjamin Macomber's *The Jewel City*, makes reference to the completion of the Panama Canal with the pronouncement, "An international exposition is a symbol of world progress. This one is so complete in its significance, so inclusive of all the best that man has done, that it is something more than a memorial of another event. It is itself epochal, as is the enterprise it commemorates." With unintended humor, Rose Berry wrote in another guidebook, *The Dream City*, of the elevating character of the architecture, sculpture, and murals at the exposition, noting that "lest all this should not hold us and something still fail, Mr.

THE TOWER OF JEWELS ILLUMINATED. REPRODUCED IN ROBERT A. REID, THE PANAMA-PACIFIC INTERNATIONAL EXPOSITION (SAN FRANCISCO, 1915). PHOTOGRAPHER UNKNOWN. COLLECTION THE AMES GALLERY, BERKELEY

Porter Garnett of Berkeley has inscribed some of the most inspired utterances from the greatest minds of the world, and when you read them they thrill and vibrate with the music of life and prophecy . . . ."[9] The decorative program itself was meant to be legible, but words were supplied for the artistically illiterate.

The Panama-Pacific Exposition was spectacular and edifying, but it wasn't all serious. Its attributes were parodied, or at least contrasted, in a large amusement area known as the Zone or the Joy Zone. As in City Beautiful plans upon which the exposition was based, this commercial space was rigorously segregated from the main fair. John Barry observed it "shrieking at you from one side" of the Fillmore Street entrance to the fair.[10] It "hardly puts you in the mood for the beauty of the courts," he concluded. Its distinctness from the rest of the fair was expressed in the variety and disorder of its architecture – it featured buildings in every conceivable style, outlined in lights and festooned with banners. It conveyed a

different tone, replacing instruction with entertainment, sobriety with levity. The zone's most important feature was a five-acre replica of the Panama Canal, but it also encompassed rides, dioramas, displays of natural oddities or medical and ethnographic curiosities, and performances by scantily clad women. It included diving girls; an exhibit on the dawn of life; a scenic railroad that passed under huge fabricated elephants; a replica of Yellowstone National Park complete with working geysers; alligator and ostrich farms; displays of premature infants in incubators; a Wild West show; and a mock-up Hopi village constructed by the Santa Fe railroad entitled "Life of a Vanishing Race." Its separateness from the rest of the exposition evidenced the planner's discomfort with what they must have judged to be its tawdriness and sensationalism, but its popularity, as at other fairs, provided much-needed revenue. It was the noisy engine that drove the larger vehicle of civic improvement.

In both its outward form and its socially constructive symbolism, the Panama-Pacific Exposition dazzled far more worldly eyes than Rizzoli's. The young Edmund Wilson wrote to a friend in 1915, "I probably shall not be able to convince you how good the Exposition is. It . . . is architecturally so successful that it at once raises the question why, if American architects can build temporary buildings as good as this, can't they build permanent ones of the same kind." Wilson went on to allude to the social ambitions of the fair, declaring, "A great lesson should be learned from this Exposition! I look forward to the regeneration of America by means of architecture."[11]

The Panama-Pacific Exposition was the last of the great Beaux-Arts fairs, but it lived on in the work of Rizzoli. Many of its structural, linguistic, and stylistic characteristics surfaced twenty years later in his plans for Y.T.T.E., which he sometimes referred to as "The Expeau of Magnitude, Magnificence, and Manifestation." He adopted its symmetrical and axial arrangement, although he added radial avenues. He placed Y.T.T.E. on the shore of an island, not in the San Francisco Bay, but in the Sea of Delicia. Like the exposition, Rizzoli's Y.T.T.E. was organized around ceremonial courts. One of them was even devoted to the four seasons – though he whimsically called the buildings that would represent them the Eager-ray, the Nevermine, the Roomiroll, and the Tootlewoo. At the Panama-Pacific Exposition, the main axis terminated at the Palace of Fine Arts, which was separated from the main body of the fair by a lagoon. In the Y.T.T.E. plot plan, something similar happens – industrial and manufacturing installations are at the terminus, divided from the remainder of the structures by military parade grounds and livestock pastures. At the crossing of the axis described by the parade grounds, just where Maybeck's temple stood in the Panama-Pacific Exposition, Rizzoli placed an enigmatic but presumably very significant element that he titled "The Dark Horse of the Festival Year."

Just as the exposition reached for exalted language in its Fountain of Energy, its Tower of Jewels, and its Court of the Universe, so Rizzoli gave resounding names to the proposed features of his plan: The Tower of Culture, the Temple of Peace, the Court of Justice. In the same way, the eclectic historicism of the fair's architecture was a point of departure for Rizzoli in his symbolic portraits and in his drawings for projected major elements of Y.T.T.E. He described *The Mailomile*, for example, one of his first symbolizations, as the "Postman . . . metamorphosed into a structure following classical proportions throughout." *The Mailomile* takes the form of an elongated Renaissance palazzo, with a rusticated lower story under a facade composed of twenty-five bays framed by freestanding Corinthian columns. Behind the columns are windows with Gothic tracery. A similar mixture of styles can be found in structures for Y.T.T.E., such as the Temple of Peace, a tower featuring Gothic fenestration and an Italianate ribbed dome, like Brunelleschi's for the Florence Cathedral. Rizzoli was even infected with the boosterism of the exposition in describing his Expeau. "It looks like the capitol of the world is in the making," he wrote on the sixth preliminary study for the Y.T.T.E. plot plan in 1940. Parodying the speech of the commercial huckster, he announced on the cover of his 1940 A.T.E. *Portfolio,* "Nothing like it ever before attempted."

Despite the similarities between Y.T.T.E. and the Panama-Pacific Exposition, Rizzoli demonstrated again that he was no mere copyist. Among the significant changes he made in the leap from Expo to Expeau was to incorporate amusements and concessions into the main body of the plan, instead of exiling them to a separate zone. Y.T.T.E. was to include an edifice called the Amusmenblock, along with a Palace of Relaxation, a Shrine of Motion Pictures, an Opera House, and a Melodeon. The tallest structure would be the Concessions and Amusement Row, which would provide "thrills judiciously produced. To have an elevation of 1000 feet at least." An area called Shops and Stores would "feature gorgeous displays of merchandise." There would be a Vitavoile of Happiness, "in which to what extent one is, or why one isn't, happy will be determined." For "the delight of infants, babes, and tots," the Babideday Fairyland would be built. For those desiring more mature entertainment, there would be La Casa del Mysteria, "in which only the most sophisticated dare undertake the experience." The Panama-Pacific Exposition allowed you just a little entertainment with your moral instruction. Y.T.T.E. reversed the equation, the better to promote elation. It was itself the Joy Zone.

True to the spirit of the Panama-Pacific Exposition, however, Rizzoli still managed to slip in some improvement with the amusement. In recognition of people's darker impulses, Y.T.T.E. included something called the Stock of Bestiality, not to mention the bug-shaped Pit of Debauchery ("in which hundreds are seen to enter and few seen to leave alive"). But Rizzoli placed a bigger emphasis on individual and social advancement. The Court of the Four Seasons was to center on the Temple of Life, depicted in a thumbnail sketch as a tiered octagonal tower over 800 feet tall, which was "to be dedicated to the theory that every individual born should be allowed to live . . . for eighty years provided he follows a certain proscribed procedure

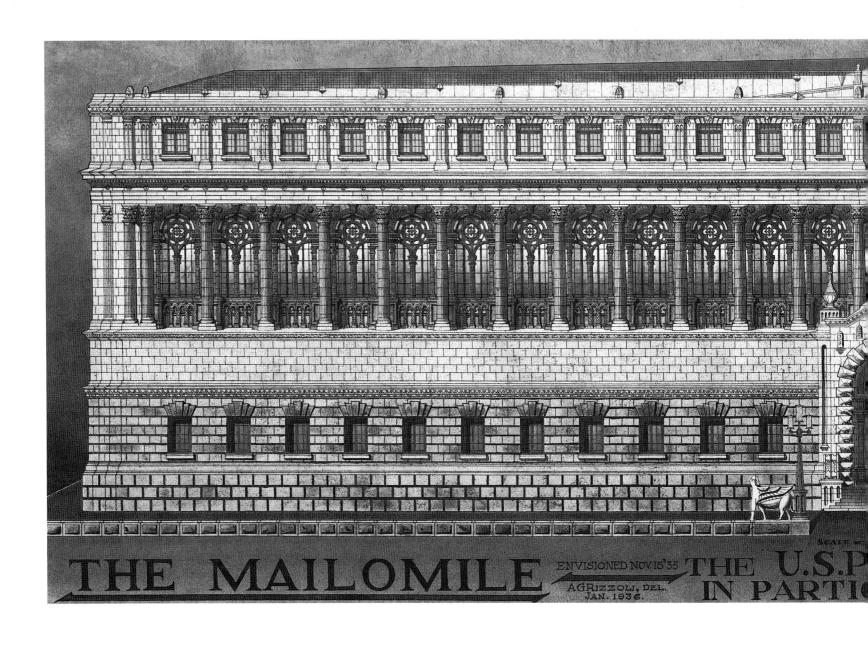

THE MAILOMILE ENVISIONED NOV.15ᵗʰ'35 THE U.S.P.
A.G.RIZZOLI, DEL.
JAN. 1936. IN PARTIC

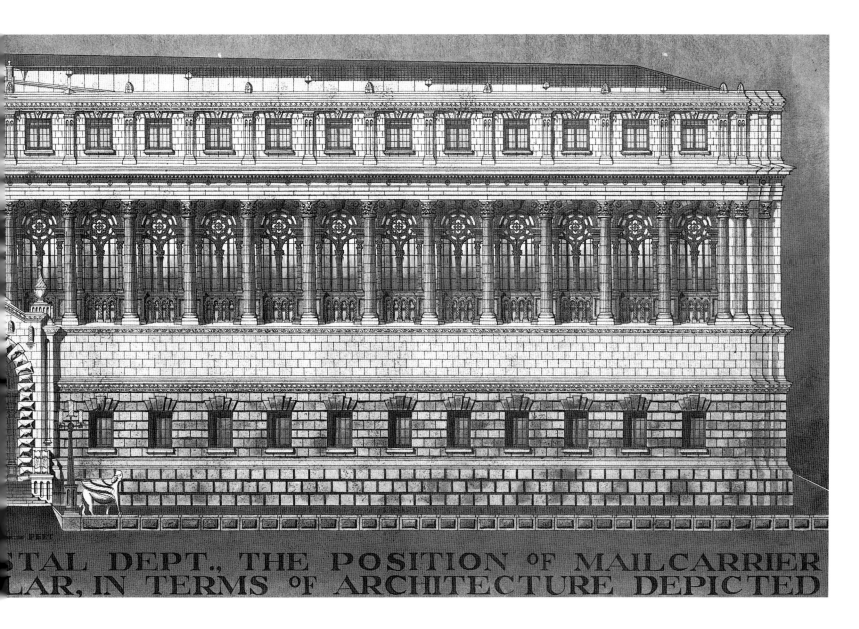

STAL DEPT., THE POSITION OF MAILCARRIER
LAR, IN TERMS OF ARCHITECTURE DEPICTED

THE MAILOMILE/THE U.S.
POSTAL DEPT.,THE POSITION OF
MAIL CARRIER IN PARTICULAR,
IN TERMS OF ARCHITECTURE
DEPICTED. 1936. INK ON RAG
PAPER, 11⅝ X 35⅜" (29.5 X
89.9 CM). COLLECTION THE
AMES GALLERY, BERKELEY

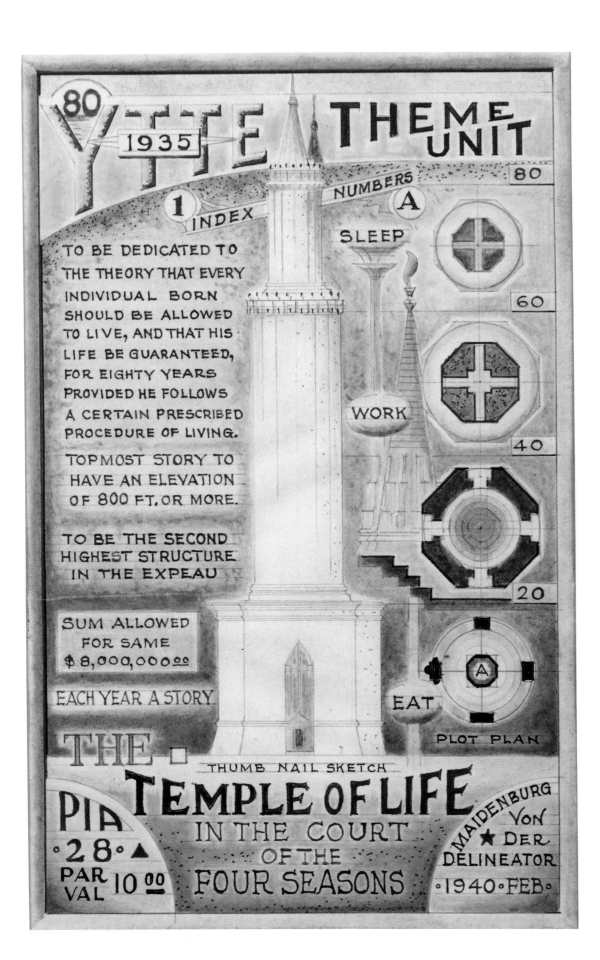

TEMPLE OF LIFE. 1940. INK ON RAG PAPER, 8⁵⁄₁₆ X 5³⁄₈" (21.1 X 13.7 CM). COLLECTION DR. SIRI VON REIS, NEW YORK

of living." The tower was interrupted with setbacks at the twentieth and sixtieth stories and terminated with a conical roof at the eightieth, representing the goal and appropriate conclusion of life in Rizzoli's scheme (the importance of this idea is suggested by the fact that A.T.E. might be a homophone for eighty).

Human relations in Y.T.T.E. would be governed by the Spirit of Cooperation, which Rizzoli depicted in a structure by the same name. One of Rizzoli's most restrained and symmetrical designs, it is a decorative structure with pairs of towers flanking a monumental court, "illustrating unmistakably the reactions to the moment there should be true harmony between firstly, man and woman, secondly, labor and capital, thirdly, states and peoples." Rizzoli admitted to some differences between these pairs, even in cooperation: the two outermost towers have different treatments in their domes and both are different from the central tower. But all are essentially classical in form, representing the goal of cooperation through a unified architectural image. (There is a hint that Rizzoli thought the Spirit of Cooperation might be a hopeless quest, however: the sponsor of this pavilion is identified on the drawing as Victor Betterlaugh.)

If you followed Rizzoli's rules for living, you would be granted a good death. Y.T.T.E. would include *The Shaft of Ascension*, where "euthanasia is available to those desiring and meriting a pleasant, painless bon voyage from this land." The structure features a series of successively taller but smaller chambers for taking leave first of the public, then friends, and finally, family. These chambers led ultimately to the Shaft of Benediction, a tower "in which life leaves the body and ascension occurs" (in what looks for all the world like an elevator). The *Shaft of Ascension* is very Beaux-Arts in plan, displaying strict bilateral symmetry and elegant proportional relationships among the parts. The section reveals a sequence of neoclassical spaces, including a colonnaded entrance, a rotunda, and an arcade. The tower itself is not detailed, but the elevation suggests it might resemble an Art Deco skyscraper (a form Rizzoli used on several occasions, as in *Mr. O. A. Deichmann's Mother Symbolically Sketched*).

Y.T.T.E. bears a closer connection to the Panama-Pacific Exposition than do other aspects of Rizzoli's work, but allusions to the fair appear in some of his symbolic portraits as well. Most conspicuous in this regard is *Mrs. Geo. Powleson Symbolically Portrayed/The Mother Tower of Jewels*. Drawn "in appreciation of her remark 'you are a jewel' uttered March 6, 1935," it was one of Rizzoli's first representations of an individual in the guise of a building. It is a close, albeit a more ornate and fanciful, approximation of the Tower of Jewels at the exposition: a triumphal arch at ground level, rising through successively smaller square, then round tiers, all embellished with columns and pilasters of every conceivable variety. The original Tower of Jewels was attached to two of the principal exhibition halls at the fair, each of which had a dome centered behind the main entrance. *Mrs. Geo. Powleson Symbolically Portrayed* retains this relationship with half domes that bracket the main arch.

As the years passed and these symbolic portraits grew more and more elaborate, they became less suggestive of the exposition. Rizzoli abandoned the fair's principles of symmetry and unity, even as he became more eclectic in his juxtapositions of historical forms and styles. This was especially true in the symbolizations he made as expressions of friendship and gratitude to the neighborhood girls who were the most reliable patrons of the A.T.E. *Grace M. Popich Symbolically Sketched*, for example, was drawn "in appreciation of the good taste she showed as she with a group of girl friends visited the A.T.E. during its second anniversary day, being the first strangers to do so." Architecturally, the portrait of Grace is completely implausible. It suggests an unlikely hybrid of London's Tower Bridge and the Coliseum in Rome, or perhaps the eighteenth-century fluted tower made to look like a fragment of a colossal column at Le désert de Retz near Paris. It is an oval structure with a pair of towers on its minor axis, which are connected by a covered walk. Other spires of

THE SPIRIT OF COOPERATION/
ACADEMICALLY THE ESSOSEE.
1935. INK ON RAG PAPER,
17⁹⁄₁₆ X 23⅝" (44.6 X 60 CM).
COLLECTION THE AMES GALLERY,
BERKELEY

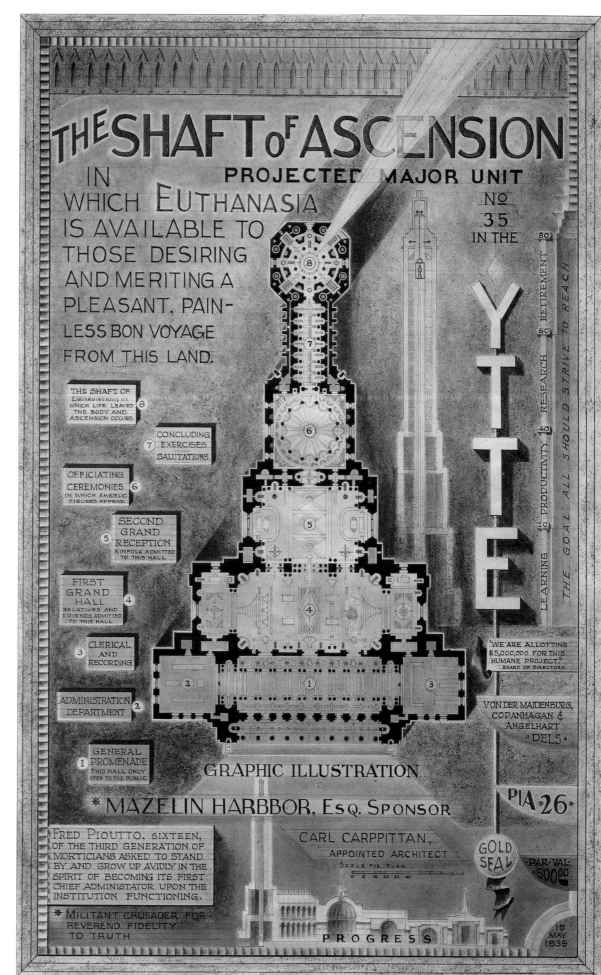

THE SHAFT OF ASCENSION.

1939. INK ON RAG PAPER,

21¹⁄₁₆ X 13" (53.5 X 33 CM).

COLLECTION THE AMES GALLERY,

BERKELEY

MRS. GEO. POWLESON SYMBOL-
ICALLY PORTRAYED/THE MOTHER
TOWER OF JEWELS. 1935.
INK ON RAG PAPER, 37 X 25⅛"
(94 X 63.8 CM). COLLECTION
PAUL GRAUBERGER, BELMONT,
CALIFORNIA

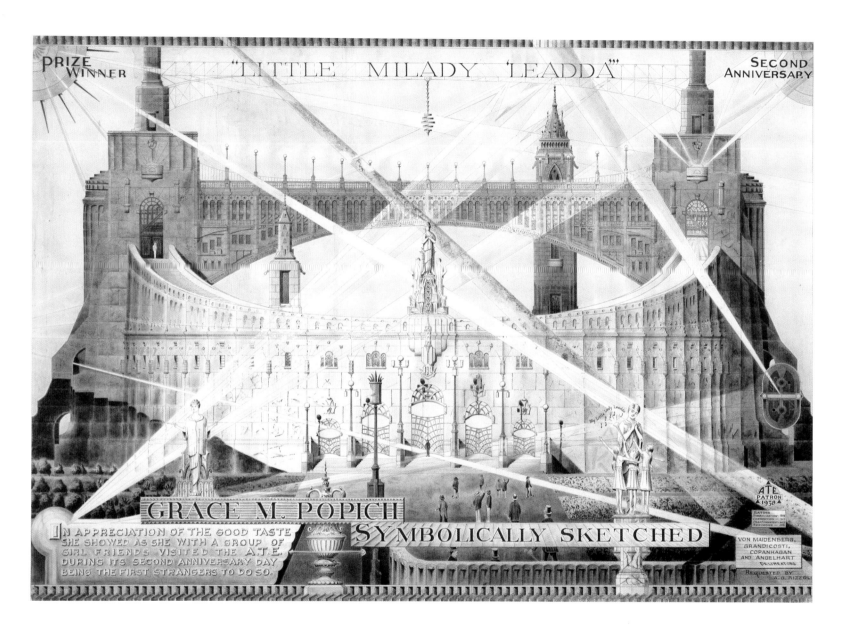

wildly divergent sizes and characters appear off center in the elevation. But the drawing continues to carry subtle reminders of the fair in the pattern of searchlights, which are reminiscent of the spectacular effects of the Scintillator.

It might seem implausible that the Panama-Pacific Exposition could stay sufficiently vivid in Rizzoli's mind to surface twenty years later in his drawings. But Rizzoli's fascination with the fair found another expression in the interval. He devoted half a dozen years in the late twenties and early thirties to writing an architectural romance called *The Colonnade*, three thousand copies of which were printed at his expense in 1933. (They remained in their original wrappers in a closet at Rizzoli's house until his stroke.) Written under the pseudonym Peter Meter-maid, the book may have been inspired by Maybeck's Palace of Fine Arts at the exposition. The novel tells the story of architect Vincent Reamer, who attempts to impress his beloved, Leadda Maullettail, by building a monumental colonnade. Maullettail is certainly an idealized version of Rizzoli's mother; Reamer is the archetypal architect who seems to be a composite of Rizzoli and his father (with a name that may allude to St. Vincent Ferrer, the patron saint of builders).

A.T.E. Portfolio — A-13
(detail: Mother of the
A.T.E.). 1940. Diazo print
on paper, 18 x 34" (45.7 x
86.4 cm). Collection The
Ames Gallery, Berkeley

Mother in Garden. 1934.
Gelatin silver print, 4³⁄₁₆ x
2⁷⁄₁₆" (10.6 x 6.2 cm).
Collection the estate of
the artist

Leadda motivates Vincent in *The Colonnade*, but she is also acknowledged as an inspiration for Rizzoli in the inception of Y.T.T.E. In the 1940 A.T.E. *Portfolio*, Rizzoli quotes her saying to Vincent, at a particularly significant juncture in the story, "Then you are afraid of maids but not o'colonnades." Rizzoli goes on to elaborate on the significance of these words both for Reamer and for himself. "Upon uttering these ten simple words Leadda made Vincent see the light of a new era which first took root in the Colonnade and which after ten odd years blossomed out vividly (?) into the glorious, all-amazing Y.T.T.E." Leadda was Vincent's girl, but Rizzoli was full of admiration and longing for her as well: "Oh, for a second Leadda Maullettail," he often wrote. Leadda and Victor subsequently became the figurative parents of all Rizzoli did. Later in the same portfolio, Leadda is identified as the mother of the A.T.E., where she is depicted alongside a drawing that is clearly based on a photo of Rizzoli's mother in a garden. Correspondingly, in one of three small drawings collectively called *The Place, The Man, The Job*, Vincent Reamer is identified as the father of the Y.T.T.E.

Rizzoli's love and admiration for his mother also found powerful expression in the symbolic portraits he made of her each year in observance of her birthday. She was personified as a cathedral (only he called it *Kathredal*), which was projected to be a major unit of Y.T.T.E. It would have a place of honor, opposite the Temple of Matrimony and just past the Vitavoile of Virginity. (All the tributes to female purity would be in the same place.) Rizzoli's symbolizations of his mother are among the few instances in which he departed completely from a classically inspired idiom. Instead, he represented his mother as a flamboyant Gothic pile, in a style associated especially with shrines built to honor the Virgin Mary. He must have felt this was particularly appropriate to his goal of "Motherhood in stone expressed." These annual symbolizations began in 1935; each represented a different elevation of the *Kathredal*. They grew in complexity as the years passed, with the most eloquent, *Mother Symbolically Recaptured*, made just after her death in 1937.

Rizzoli's first *Kathredal*, which depicts the south elevation, shows the main entrance flanked by two very mismatched towers which are not on axis with each other. By 1937, *The Kathredal* had sprouted two more towers, one at the crossing (where you might expect it) and another – even bigger – off the apse at the northwest corner (where you definitely would not). Seemingly inspired by the Duomo in Milan, Rizzoli's *Kathredal* features enough bays, buttresses (both straight and curved, engaged and flying), spires, sculptures, glass, tracery, and finials to keep an army of artists and masons busy for centuries. It is a composite of every medieval ornament known to mankind, with a few modern ones thrown in for good measure. In the water garden that surrounds it – one of Rizzoli's few elaborate landscapes – there are pools with fountains and electric light gems, the latter once again evoking the Tower of Jewels. For full sensory effect, there is even a smoking pillar identified as a "fragrant vapors plant." Curiously, the main axis of Rizzoli's *Kathredal* ran north-south instead of east-west, with the main entrance at the south instead of the west end. Rizzoli had never seen the great cathedrals of Europe firsthand, which invariably face east toward the Holy Land. But he was seldom in error in his knowledge of architectural example. Was this an inadvertent or a deliberate change from the historical model? Rizzoli was a Catholic who grew increasingly devout in his later years; he was baptized in 1952. He may have felt it was blasphemous to propose a cathedral to his mother that conformed in every particular to its prototype.

1937

MOTHER SYMBOLICALLY
RECAPTURED/THE KATHREDAL.
1937. INK ON RAG PAPER,
30⅛ x 50¼" (76.5 x 127.6 CM).
COLLECTION THE AMES GALLERY,
BERKELEY

How did Rizzoli hit on the idea of using architectural form to portray the important people in his life? One of the fixtures of Beaux-Arts architectural theory was the idea that buildings should be outwardly expressive of their inner character, revealing something of both their spatial organization and their program in external details. They should be appropriate in scale and ornament to their use and give some indication of the nature and importance of their purpose. The notion of character derived ultimately from the classical conception of "decorum" – the idea, conveyed by Horace in his *Ars Poetica*, that each person represented in art should demonstrate a character appropriate to his type. Although the implications of decorum for architecture were first addressed by Vitruvius, it was in the eighteenth century that the expression of character became of great theoretical concern, especially for the academicians Germaine Boffrand (1667–1754) and J.-F. Blondel (1705–74). Boffrand maintained in his *Livre d'Architecture*, for example, that "Different buildings by their layout, by their structure, and by the manner in which they are decorated ought to tell the spectator their purpose, and if they do not do so, they transgress against expression and are not what they ought to be."[12]

The expression of character was most often achieved through imitation of the important historical precedents for any given type of building, or by attaching appropriate symbols or decorations – carving the names of artists on a museum or affixing a lyre to a theater, for example. But the late-eighteenth-century French architect Claude-Nicolas Ledoux (1736–1806) and others of his era, including the otherwise very distinct designers Etienne-Louis Boullée (1728–1799) and Jean-Jacques Lequeu (1757–ca.1825), experimented with giving structure itself such a form that it might reveal the purpose of a building. Their revolutionary designs were described as *architecture parlante*, or narrative architecture. The term, first applied in the nineteenth century to describe the work of Ledoux, implied that buildings could bespeak their character through specific allusions to function. Lequeu pushed these ideas in possibly the most fanciful direction – one of the most familiar instances of *architecture parlante* is the drawing he made for a cowshed in the form of a cow, but he also designed an oracular temple atop a grotto with a keyhole-shaped opening, a gate to a hunting park formed with the heads of boars and stags, and a monument to Priapus with a cock's head, a human neck, and a tumescent male member for a nose.[13]

Equally as relevant to Rizzoli as the ideas of *architecture parlante* are the connections that have long been drawn between architecture and the human body. Ever since Vitruvius, it has been a truism of classical architecture that its proportions are derived from those of mankind. This notion is visualized most obviously in the caryatid, the figure-as-column. By legend, the various orders were gender-derived – the Doric from the male body, the Ionic and Corinthian from the female. In the eighteenth century, architecture was also linked to physiognomy – the pseudoscience in which human character was believed to be evident in a person's physical features. The study of physiognomy is probably most familiar in art through the work of the seventeenth-century French court painter Charles Le Brun, who executed a series of drawings of different facial expressions, each indicating a different character or personality type. Ideas about physiognomy were subsequently applied to architecture in the writings of Nicolas Le Camus de Mézières (1721–ca.1793), author of a treatise called *Le Génie de l'architecture* (1780). Le Camus insisted that "every object possesses a character, proper to it alone, and that often a single line, a plain contour will suffice to express it." Just as the faces of the lion, the tiger, or the leopard "are composed of lines that make them terrible and strike fear into the boldest hearts," so the form of inanimate objects can provoke our feelings. "A structure catches the eye by virtue of its mass; its general outline attracts or repels us. When we look at a building," Le Camus observed, "our sensations are of contradictory kinds: gaiety in one place, despondency in another. One sensation induces quiet reflection, another inspires awe or maintains respect."[14]

Eighteenth-century ideas about *architecture parlante* and the connections between physiognomy and architecture might seem remote from Rizzoli, but they survived into the twentieth century. They turn up in a book that Rizzoli recommended in his 1940 *A.T.E. Portfolio*: Howard Robertson's *Modern Architectural Design* (1932). The book contains an entire chapter on "Expression," which Robertson defines firstly as "the outward manifestation of the inner purpose of the building, i.e., the characterization of the building programme." The real task of a designer, Robertson maintains, is "to use his knowledge of certain aids to effect, and of practical details, to lend his design distinction of character and an expressive physiognomy." After defining physiognomy, Robertson continues – very much in the spirit of Le Camus – to insist that "Arched eyebrows give to the human expression an air of interrogation, or surprise, sometimes of superciliousness or aristocratic aloofness. Arched openings, at the top of a façade, frequently convey a similar expression. Square shapes, strong rigid lines, imply firmness, as do also bold projections. Wavy lines, delicate reeded profiles, suggest grace and elegance, as do slender proportions in general.

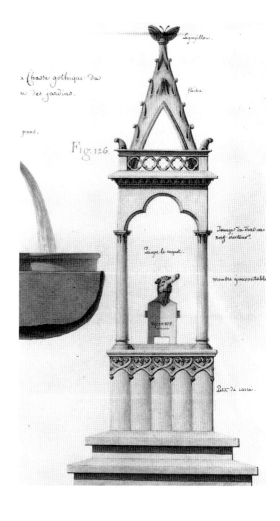

ABOVE: JEAN-JACQUES LEQUEU. PRIAPUS. FROM ARCHITECTURE CIVILE (CIVIL ARCHITECTURE). C. 1825. COLLECTION BIBLIOTHÈQUE NATIONALE DE FRANCE

JEAN-JACQUES LEQUEU. L'ETABLE VACHE (THE COWSHED). FROM ARCHITECTURE CIVILE (CIVIL ARCHITECTURE). C. 1825. COLLECTION BIBLIOTHÈQUE NATIONALE DE FRANCE

The human countenance," Robertson concludes, "is an excellent guide in respect of the reactions of form on expression of character, and the architect has a whole fund of observation on humanity to assist him."[15]

In pronounced ways, Rizzoli's designs are consistent with general ideas about *architecture parlante* and more specific theories of physiognomy and architecture. In his proposals for Y.T.T.E., both the overall plan and the individual elements seem intended to speak. The plan, while bearing analogies to the layout of the Panama-Pacific Exposition, also resembles a cathedral, which would suggest an intention to evoke the New Jerusalem or the City of God. It is clearly, in Rizzoli's phrase, "a bit of heavenly architecture." In the same way, individual elements of Y.T.T.E. were designed to convey a distinct character. The

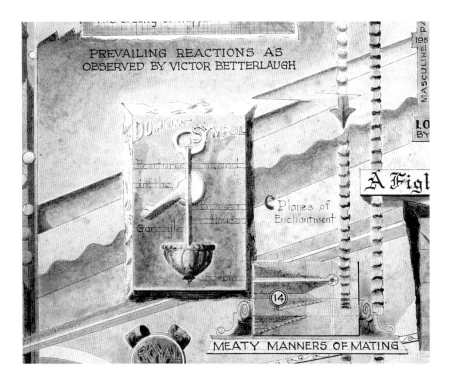

THE BLUESEA HOUSE (DETAIL
OF BARBIN AND GARGOYLE).
1938. INK ON RAG PAPER,
20⅜ X 30⅜" (51.8 X 77.2 CM).
COLLECTION MICHAEL GROSSMAN,
NEW YORK

balanced form of *The Spirit of Cooperation* was meant to convey exactly this; and the splendor of the *Kathredal* to express reverence for virtuous motherhood. The bug-shaped Pit of Debauchery, on the other hand, spoke to the lower forms of life.

Rizzoli was also attentive to the ways architectural character might convey gender distinctions. The *Kathredal* was conceptualized as a feminine edifice because of its associations with Marian worship. Elsewhere, there were specifically masculine buildings, such as the *Veeaye/The Ornament*. Based on the earlier *Primalglimse*, this was rendered as a towering structure that expressed the turbulent feelings elicited in Rizzoli by the feminine form ("the most amazing thing in life and yet the least known"). Y.T.T.E. was also to include a structure called the Toure of Phallism (later the Beauty of Phallism); although Rizzoli left no elevations for this building, we can well imagine what it might have resembled. Rizzoli also carried these gender distinctions into his decorative program: in a detail of *Bluesea House*, his rendering on the "meaty manners of mating," the gargoyle and the barbin (or basin) are identified as the "dominant symbol featured on and in the Bluesea House," representing masculine and feminine character, respectively. Curiously, the basin appears on top of the fluted and distinctly phallic tower that dominates Rizzoli's symbolic portrait of Gerry Holt, as if he felt Holt combined the best attributes of men and women.

But Rizzoli turns the notion of architectural physiognomy on its ear. Instead of looking to the human countenance as a source of expressive form in architecture, Rizzoli was looking to the conventions of architectural form for analogies to the character he perceived in his human subjects. On one level, Rizzoli was playing a game in these symbolizations, in which he could express his vision of others in a coded language that was outwardly familiar but deeply personal in its individual permutations. As with all of Rizzoli's fun, however, this tactic had its more hidden and poignant aspects. He was using the language he knew well – architecture – to explore a phenomenon he seems hardly to have known at all –

GERRY GEORGE GOULD HOLT/
THE "CADEVTR." 1940. INK
ON RAG PAPER, 36 X 25¾"
(91.4 X 65.4 CM). COLLECTION
THE AMES GALLERY, BERKELEY

interpersonal relationships. These elliptical portraits of friends and acquaintances suggest that the deeper dimensions of human interaction and emotion remained a mystery to him, one he could only approach through the medium of architecture. His drawings were not only an antidote to loneliness, but also the expression of it.

Rizzoli's general familiarity with historical form and more particular knowledge of narrative architecture raises tantalizing questions about how familiar he might have been with the specific details of visionary schemes by eighteenth-century architects associated with *architecture parlante*. There are some uncanny similarities between Rizzoli's ideas and those of Ledoux in particular. In the fifteen years prior to his death in 1806, Ledoux developed plans for an ideal town to surround the Royal Saltworks at Arc and Senans (not far from Besançon), which had been built to his designs in the latter half of the 1770s. Although these plans remained hypothetical, they were highly intricate and published in the first volume of an 1804 treatise ponderously titled *L'architecture considérée sous le rapport de l'art, des moeurs, et de la législation*. The

town, to be called Chaux after a nearby forest, was to take the form of a perfect circle with the saltworks at the center; additional public and private buildings would extend outward along radial avenues into the countryside. But the town was more than a formal exercise. It was intended to demonstrate Ledoux's concern with providing artistic solutions for social problems – alleviating rural poverty; instituting agricultural reform; improving health, sanitation, and education; and planning for industrial development.[16]

Most pertinent to the work of Rizzoli, the town was to include a number of structures devoted to spiritual welfare, including several moralizing institutions. One was to be called the Panarèthéon, a neologism referring to the building's function as a school of morality. Another was the House of Union, an emblem of brotherhood and the importance of social cohesion. The Temple of Memory would honor women as public and private heroines, as the bearers of natural virtues. At the other extreme, the Oikéma, a public brothel, would insure the sanctity of matrimony in a roundabout way – by allowing young men

Vue perspective de la Ville de Chaux

PL. 116

CLAUDE-NICOLAS LEDOUX. **PERSPECTIVE VIEW OF THE TOWN OF CHAUX**. ENGRAVING BY BERTHAULT FROM DANIEL RAMÉE, **ARCHITECTURE DE C-N LEDOUX** (PARIS: LENOIR ÉDITEUR, 1847), PL. 116.

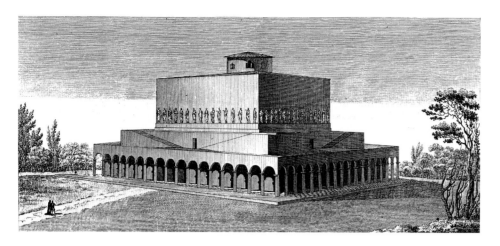

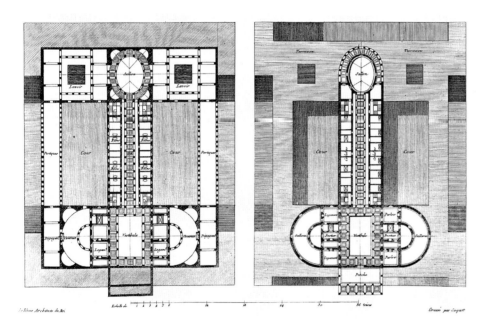

to experience the pleasures of the flesh to libertine excess, after which, utterly satiated, they were sure to settle peacefully into the stability of marriage.

In the manner of narrative architecture, these buildings were to reveal their purpose in outward appearance. The House of Union would express social coherence through its cubic form and central plan; it would mirror the symmetry and concentric organization of the larger plan for Chaux. The Temple of Memory would feature cylindrical towers at each corner, embellished with bas-reliefs detailing the virtuous deeds of women. (Ledoux seems to have conceived of this temple both as a shrine to motherhood and as a tribute to his own mother.) The many levels of the Panarèthéon suggested the ascent toward enlightenment; allegorical sculptures on the outside constituted a veritable catalogue of admirable characteristics. Ledoux's most extreme instance of narrative architecture for Chaux is found in the house of sexual initiation, the plan of which clearly resembles an erect phallus.

While there are general analogies between the idealism of Ledoux's town and Rizzoli's Expeau, it is in the specific application of narrative schemes to structures for moral improvement that Rizzoli's ambitions for Y.T.T.E. most clearly coincide with Ledoux's for Chaux. There are even resemblances in the details: between the central plan of Ledoux's House of Union and the symmetry of Rizzoli's *Spirit of Cooperation*; between Ledoux's tribute to motherhood and Rizzoli's; and between the phallic emblems of each. There are also arresting similarities between some of Lequeu's narrative designs and elements of the Y.T.T.E. Lequeu's cowshed, for example, finds a parallel in Rizzoli's proposal for a monument to the cow, called the Bossiroam ("Miss Bellarosa, sponsor and active director"). Similarly, Rizzoli's tribute to the Beauty of Phallism is a cousin to Lequeu's monument to Priapus as much as to Ledoux's Oikéma. If Rizzoli knew anything about Lequeu, he might have felt a special kinship with him. A lowly draftsman who thought of himself on a par with the better-known architects of his generation, Lequeu is remembered not for his commissioned work but for the architectural fantasies he drew in his spare time. He was fascinated with his own physiognomy and its application to architecture; he even created a treatise on facial representation.

But it is unlikely that Rizzoli was familiar with either Ledoux or Lequeu – little published material on their work was available in this country until the 1950s.[17] The similarities between Rizzoli's work and theirs is probably less the expression of direct influence than of the remarkable tenacity of Beaux-Arts ideas about architectural narrative and character, which became widely dispersed through the nineteenth century – albeit in a watered-down fashion. Rizzoli might not have known of Ledoux's plans for Chaux, for example, but he might have seen more recent Beaux-Arts efforts to visualize ideal towns, such as Ernest Hébrard's drawings for "A World Centre of Communication." This was a hypothetical city with cultural, scientific, and athletic facilities designed to improve international relations, the plans for which were published in the United States in 1913.[18] Even if Rizzoli had known of Lequeu or Ledoux, he wasn't apt to let on. He liked to make extravagant claims for his work ("Nothing like it ever before attempted"). The Bossiroam, he maintained on the 1938 plot plan, was "Honoring, for the First Time in History, The Cow." In the same vein, he insisted that the Beauty of Phallism had "the Most Novel Derivation in Architecture, Inspired by a Flea Bite."

In one way, however, it seems clear that Rizzoli *was* patterning himself on his predecessors. Beaux-Arts architectural education was based on treatises written by eighteenth-century architects. Like Ledoux and Lequeu, Boullée and Le Camus, Rizzoli was the author of an elaborate architectural discourse. His consisted of over five hundred sheets, of which some three hundred and fifty survive. Most are divided into eight separate pages; collectively they carry thousands of individual poems and drawings. Rizzoli's treatise was envisioned as a third book of the Christian Bible and was an expression of his devotion both to architecture and to God. Indeed, it was his assertion of the absolute indivisibility of the two. In an introduction to the text, which he called by various titles, including *The A.M.T.E. Celestial Extravaganza: "Poetry in Architecture,"* he explained that his purpose was "to show the affinity existing between architecture and theology, or looking to God as the fountainhead of all creation. A relationship which seems, to this person after many years

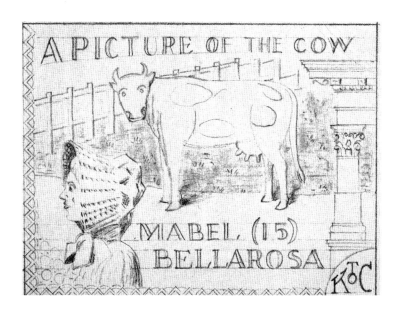

MR. AND MRS. HAROLD HEALY
SYMBOLICALLY SKETCHED/
FIRST PRIZE, FIRST ANNIVER-
SARY. 1936. INK ON RAG
PAPER, 35½ x 24⅝" (90.2 x
62.6 CM). COLLECTION THE
AMES GALLERY, BERKELEY

of meditation and experimentation, to be quite unseparable." As with his drawings, Rizzoli's treatise was created with many supposed collaborators, some of whom were apparently his female alter egos: principally, a character named Miss Amte, but also Rechi Tacteur and Marilyn Architecteur. (In the eighteenth century, Lequeu often portrayed himself as a woman; in the twentieth, so did the French artist Marcel Duchamp.) Throughout, Rizzoli invokes artists and architects, statesmen, saints, popes, philosophers, and engineers to lend his text an air of expertise. But Rizzoli's real claim to authority came from the fact that he was "being guided by divine providence"; he was the "architectural transcriber to God."

The treatise contains testimony to disturbing visions. This has confirmed for some observers what they had already deduced from his drawings: that Rizzoli was mentally ill. One writer even went so far as to diagnose Rizzoli as schizophrenic.[19] But we should be cautious of the now too casual linking of creativity and madness. Art is at least as much a product of outward as inward circumstance, expressing social and cultural conditioning as much as individual mental health. We have a tendency to characterize conduct as ill simply because it deviates from what society determines to be the norm at any given time. This is especially true of idiosyncratic devotional behavior – intense personal faith, such as Rizzoli demonstrated in his treatise, is sometimes taken as a sign of mental disorder. But in the absence of any clinical diagnosis, it does more harm than good to insist that Rizzoli was mentally ill. It stigmatizes him, marginalizes his work, and denies his evident connections to his cultural sources, among them the Roman Catholic church, the traditions of Beaux-Arts rendering and design, the notions of architectural character and physiognomy, and the social ambitions of the City Beautiful Movement. Moreover, it is contrary to the testimony of his colleagues. Gerry Holt says Rizzoli was "definitely not crazy. He was very matter-of-fact." Violetta

Autumn, a retired architect who worked with Rizzoli in Deichmann's office for a few months in 1954, is more equivocal. "I thought maybe he was a little mad. He had a reality of his own; he lived two lives." But she confirms that he functioned well at work. She remembers him "sitting at his dusty desk for hours drawing rustications," the decorative details of Deichmann's buildings.

Admittedly, Rizzoli had emotional difficulties. He was a lonely man with an attachment to his mother that is not normative today; based on visual and textual evidence, he was erotically repressed and conflicted. But we should be prepared to empathize with these difficulties, not label them. I suggested at the outset that 1915 was the crucial year in Rizzoli's emotional and artistic life; that the death of his father and the joyous occasion of the Panama-Pacific Exposition became linked in his mind, the one the inverse of the other. It was the year things fell apart for Rizzoli; it was also the year in which he grabbed on to his vision of a more perfect world, a world of total elation, perhaps as a compensation for his loss. Y.T.T.E. became his answer to loneliness, but it may also have represented the symbolic reconstruction of his family. His visionary Expeau is as much a tribute to his father as to his mother, I think. They are its two patrons; it has its shrines to both of them. The *Kathredal* is the homage to his mother. The tribute to his father is less evident, but I suspect it is the element never drawn in elevation but always highlighted in the plans, called *The Dark Horse of the Festival Year*. As is the case with so many of Rizzoli's titles, this probably has several meanings, all somewhat obscure. On the one hand it might allude to the dark occurrence of the festival year; on the other, it might suggest the eventual triumph of his father – his restoration to a rightful place in the family through his anticipated resurrection in the promised land.

Rizzoli's work is rife with allusions to a strong masculine presence – in all the phallic constructions most obviously, but also in the substantiality of images such as *Irwin Peter Sicotte, Jr., Symbolically Delineated*, in which the edifice springs from solid rock. His drawings also convey an idealized and hierarchical vision of family structure, with a powerful male at the heart of a stable group. Both *Mr. and Mrs. Harold Healy* and *Alfredo Capobianco and Family* reveal this vision. In each, the male is represented by an ornamented tower that dominates the middle of the composition, flanked by successively smaller depictions of other members of the family. In the rendering of the Healy family, the wife is portrayed in the cylindrical edifice to the right, while the plain elements to the left depict a presumably rather nondescript cousin who accompanied the Healys on their visit to the A.T.E. In giving primacy to the male, Rizzoli may simply have been expressing social conventions. But the sense of loneliness and longing that pervade his work make it seem that he was representing in these renderings the ideal family that he lost early or perhaps never had, with a strong father at the center.

But why, beyond chronological coincidence, did the fair become linked with the death of his father? Trauma has a way of creating fixations; it can also have a paradoxical effect, bringing out latent powers that might not otherwise emerge. The neurologist Oliver Sacks, in a collection of essays, *An Anthropologist on Mars*, says that "For me, as a physician, nature's richness is to be studied in the phenomena of health and disease, in the endless forms of individual adaptation by which human organisms, people, adapt and reconstruct themselves, faced with the challenges and vicissitudes of life." He suggests that the brain is remarkably plastic, "a supremely adaptive system geared for evolution and change, ceaselessly adapting to the needs of the organism – its need, above all, to construct a coherent self and world . . ." This adaptability is so striking, Sacks says, that he is "sometimes moved to wonder whether it may not be necessary to redefine the very concepts of 'health' and 'disease,' to see these in terms of the ability of the organism to create a new organization and order, one that fits its special, altered disposition and needs, rather than in the terms of a rigidly defined 'norm'". Out of the dark occurrence of the festival year, Rizzoli created both the plans and the elevations for his

new order, one in which he pictured a more coherent world for himself and for his family. Seen in the light of Sacks's meditations, Rizzoli's drawings become the expression not of illness but of health. They convey his longing for happiness – for an intact family, for companionship, for the visible communication of spirituality, and for a more perfect dominion. If this is madness, we are truly lost.

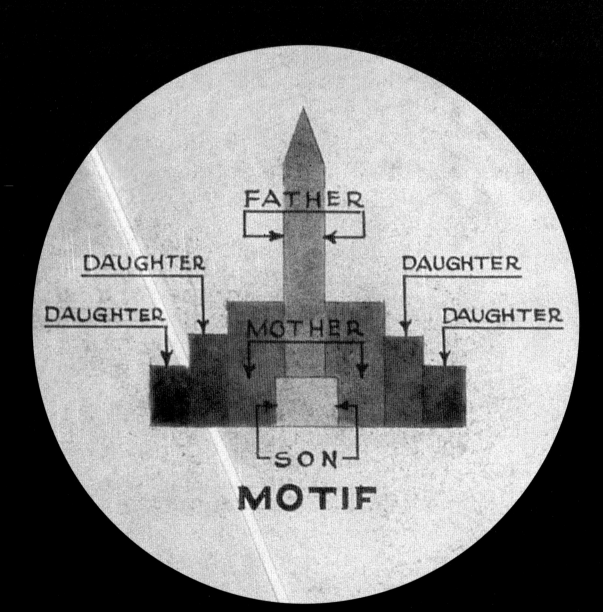

ACHILLES RIZZOLI

DRAFTSMAN AND SCRIBE

BY ROGER CARDINAL

ALFREDO CAPOBIANCO AND FAMILY SYMBOLICALLY SKETCHED/ PALAZZO DEL CAPOBIANCO (DETAIL). 1937

The extravagant visual and verbal output of Achilles G. Rizzoli might seem a unique aberration within twentieth-century culture were it not that a group of comparable creators has emerged within the category of Outsider Art to which he is now commonly assigned. To cite the names of such exemplary figures as Adolf Wölfli, Aloïse Corbaz, August Klett (known as August Klotz), Émile Josome Hodinos, Madge Gill, and Henry Darger alongside that of Rizzoli is to outline a distinctive class of artists. As befits an Outsider, each of these creators operated outside the compass of normal cultural and artistic practice; equally, each produced a lifetime's corpus of work, serially adumbrated and shaped by a stylistic and narrative matrix that facilitated delirious extrapolations of a grandiose and often transcendental character. Each can be said to confirm the profile of the obsessional picto-scriptural mythographer, one who devotes a period of decades to documenting a vast imaginary realm impressed with private meanings, while the resulting art is tellingly shaped by the intimate reciprocity of its pictorial and textual components.[1]

Whether such Outsiders are indeed pursued by the same *horror vacuui* that psychiatry has long attributed to a supposed schizophrenic style, or whether the very survival of their artistic and spiritual project depends on its being emphasized and validated at each and every point, it is certainly remarkable how they concur in dwelling industriously over their works, and, most intriguingly, in supplementing iconographic formations with a compulsive supply of text, whether in the form of inspired writings separately composed, or of inscriptions directly entered upon the picture surface. Achilles Rizzoli, as a quite prolific composer of poems and of prose fiction (albeit only one novel, *The Colonnade*, saw print, and seems never to have entered the public domain), and as a specialist of annotated architectural designs, represents a significant instance of dual-media expression within the field of Outsider Art. This essay explores the expressions of this writer-draftsman, and speculates upon the patterns and motives that inform his creative sensibility.

Let me start by considering Rizzoli's most eloquent innovation, the procedure whereby a person is, in his own words, "symbolically sketched," "represented," or "recaptured," which is to say: emblematized in the shape of a specimen of visionary architecture. The first instances of this procedure constitute the "Kathredal" cycle dedicated to Rizzoli's beloved mother. As viewers of these splendid designs, we are, I take it, intended to interpret the proliferation of slender spires and intricate adornments as so many equivalents for the spiritual qualities of the loved one – her delicacy, refinement, tenderness, and so forth. The emotional tribute which Rizzoli pays to his dead mother in *Mother Symbolically Recaptured*, on the occasion of the first birthday following her death, can be measured by the way the west elevation of a massive cathedral – or rather "The Kathredal" – bristles with pinnacles, flying buttresses, windows, catwalks, and over fifty slender statues. As architecture, it is visionary to the point of ignoring the world of material possibility. As symbolic portrayal, it is an exercise in hyperbole that amplifies filial adoration to an almost pathological degree.

Given the excessive ornamentation on so many of his symbolic buildings, it is remarkable that Rizzoli seems never to have been content to let the pictorial statement stand in its own right. He is very much like Wölfli in refusing to let well enough alone: he loves to review the finished piece, to muse upon it, to tinker a little longer. First, he feels he has to "finalize" the pictorial space by punctuating its vacancies with emblems or devices, such as stars, hearts, rosettes, or wind roses. These he wraps about by drawing ribbon borders or simulated frames, including repeated patterns resembling tiling or fancy brickwork, or, in one case, drapes set to either side of the image (*Margaret E. Griffin Symbolically Sketched*). The second manifestation of the "tinkering" impulse is one I particularly wish to highlight, namely the recourse to verbal embellishment.

Ordinarily, we expect the plans and sketches of a professional architectural draftsman to contain such marginalia as a title, a legend listing technical features, a scale to indicate spatial dimensions, the draftsman's name, the date, and so forth. To a degree, Rizzoli's additions conform to this code, but only to transgress it with a whole array of eccentric excesses. Not a single drawing is released without a freight of textual extras: secondary titles, captions, commentaries, mottoes, injunctions, acknowledgments, and fussy afterthoughts, all inscribed in insistent capitals.[2] Rizzoli is quite simply a manic of the supplement, as if obsessed by the thought that any viewer might come away unsated from the image. Fully to consume one of his drawings is to absorb a host of textual amplifications, the garrulous expressions of an anxious scribe who seems incapable of trusting the impact of his own draftsmanship.

Rizzoli's love of annotation marks one of his simpler images, the postcard-sized *Virginia Gingerbred*. What is in effect a literal, if caricatural, portrait of a ginger-haired girl with a braid is presented as an encircled profile (as if on a medallion or a postage stamp), and then given a square frame of parallel lines. Each corner of the completed image contains an insert: the date ("12.24.43"); the so-called par value of the piece (ten dollars); its allotted number in the "Piafore" series ("Pia 43"); and the delineator's name, that of one of the absurd collaborators Rizzoli so loved to invent ("Babe Ilamme Angelhart Delineator"). The effect of such appendices is to qualify the high spirits of the portrait, as if Rizzoli meant to remind the viewer of his adult commitment to precision and order (while in fact, we suspect, still indulging in disordered fantasies about the girl): here, we might say that the scribe seeks to be the moral guardian of the impulsive draftsman.

Consider an image from the symbolization series, *Virginia Tamke Symbolically Represented*. This suave rendering of an elegant, slender tower in white marble attracts no less than eight separate legends. The main title is entered in ornate serif capitals (with an eye-catching curve on the first name) within a rectangular box at the picture's base. Along the top edge of this box, and slightly jutting over its edge, is a subtitle, "The Tower of the Hour." Placed within inverted quotation marks, the formula seems designed to suggest a widely voiced opinion as to the attractiveness and timeliness of the structure (thus encouraging the inference that it might play a key part in the Y.T.T.E. project, the eventual outcome of Rizzoli's architectural fantasies). Below the topmost edge of this very tall picture, a bold hint is given as to how the viewer might decode the symbolism of the tower, namely as redolent of "Inspirational qualities she already possesses." As if to squeeze in an all but censored afterthought, the scribe allows himself a heartfelt prayer at the bottom rim of the image: "May the maiden she remain forever." (Another reference to "the 1st 20 yrs." probably reflects

Rizzoli's habit of monitoring the attractiveness of his young girl friends as they grew older; an entry in the *A.T.E. Portfolio* indicates that Virginia Tamke was eight at the time of composition.) All of these inscriptions may be seen to extrapolate from the basic equation of tower and girl, spelling out those supplementary qualities – Virginia is virginal, inspirational, otherworldly, and so forth – that might otherwise escape note. (Without delving just yet into Rizzoli's erotic subcode, I should add that, placed at bottom right of the *Tamke* image, a naked female with outstretched arms anticipates a more streamlined nude in the 1936 drawing *Gigantic Symbolic Figure [. . .] atop the Ornament . . . .*, where we encounter Rizzoli's dream of a revolving statue set atop the spire of "The Ornament," a temple in turn symbolizing another young girl of his acquaintance, Virginia Ann Entwistle, celebrated as Belladora Blossomhart, "10 and cute.")

Despite these telltale signs of emotional investment, the remaining inscriptions in the *Tamke* image that reflect the scruples of the architectural draftsman should not be overlooked. The picture is labeled "East Elevation," and a scale index (albeit made up of an eccentric thirteen intervals) enables us to calculate its height as around 235 feet. Rizzoli's name and the date (entered in quasi Deco capitals: "AGRIZZOLI, DEL. DEC. 1935"), along with a gesture toward copyright ("Original idea registered Jan. 7, 1935"), speak of a rather naive wish to confirm architectural credentials. I believe we are meant to admire not only the person of the symbolic portrait but the professional artistry of her transfiguration.

If it is true that Rizzoli courts our admiration for his technical work, he frequently makes solemn obeisance to an imaginary team of which he sees himself, presumably, as a junior member. For example, the superbly executed *The Y.T.T.E. Plot Plan: Third Preliminary Study*, is attributed in one corner to "Grandicosti, Rizzoli & Copanhagen,

SOUVENIR WINNER

... OF THE PALACE GOD IS BUILDING FOR THAT
NO LESS A PEARL EVEN FOR

PIANISSIMO

MARGARET E. GRIFFIN

SYMBOL

GIVING FORM AND COLOR TO OUR
IMPRESSION OF THE LEADING
VISITOR TO THE A·T·E· DURING ITS
3RD ANNIVERSARY DAY, AUG 7, 1938.

A
SEPTEMBER
MORN
GIRL

L·D·I

PALAZZO PIANIS

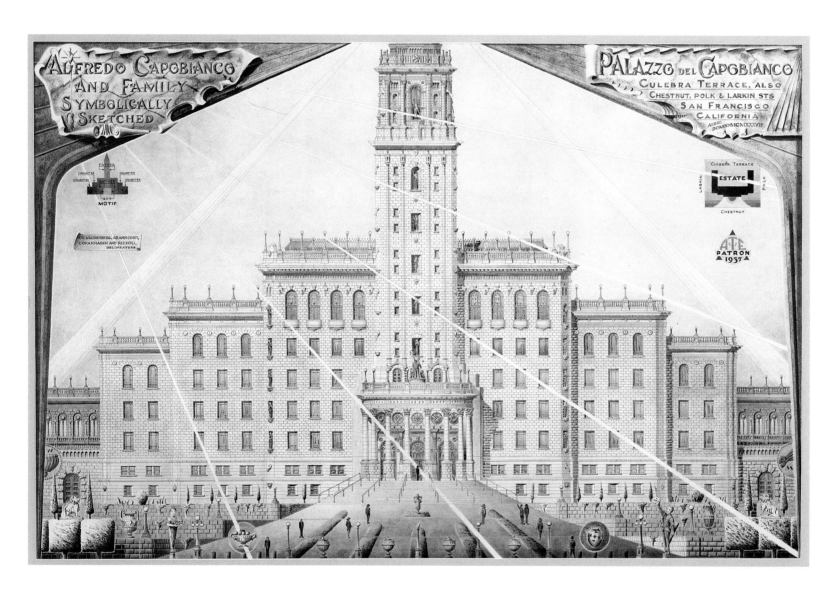

ALFREDO CAPOBIANCO AND
FAMILY SYMBOLICALLY
SKETCHED/PALAZZO DEL
CAPOBIANCO. 1937. INK ON
RAG PAPER, 24⁵⁄₁₆ X 38⁵⁄₁₆"
(62.4 X 97.3 CM). COLLEC-
TION THE AMES GALLERY,
BERKELEY

VIRGINIA GINGERBRED. 1943.
INK ON RAG PAPER, 5½ x 4½"
(14 x 11.4 CM). COLLECTION
DR. SIRI VON REIS, NEW YORK

VIRGINIA TAMKE SYMBOLICALLY
REPRESENTED/"THE TOWER OF
THE HOUR." 1935. INK ON RAG
PAPER, 33⅝ x 11¾" (85.4 x
29.9 CM). COLLECTION HELENE
AND DAVID MINTZ

Delineators," and credited in another to "Mark Marshoalla, Director-in-Chief. Vincent Reamer, Architect-in-Chief. Grainmill & Oppalleene, Associated." In one of its several legends, the highly ornate *Abraham N. Zachariah Symbolically Sketched* is ascribed to an impressive team of delineators, listed in order of seniority: "Von der Maidenburg, 56/ Victor Grandicosti, 48/ Carl Copanhagan, 45/ Babe Angelhart, 40/ Joyce Bellarosa, 25." Here we note Rizzoli's own name within a key-shaped inset at bottom right, labeled with his special function as "Curator," alongside his intertwined initials. A note, typically drawn so as to resemble a label subsequently pasted onto the finished design, reads: "Symbolization 90%; Composition 80%; Design 50%; Draftsmanship 50%; Rendering 40%." Whereupon yet another label imposes a strict ruling: "Penalyzed. Nov. 26/39. Rating for design reduced 10%, with the admonition that unless he does better next time he shall be dismissed from the staff of delineators," an interjection which, if credited to Rizzoli as quality assessor, speaks volumes about his real-life experience in the San Francisco architectural office of Otto Deichmann and associates, where he toiled for many years.

It can happen that Rizzoli's pretentions to grandeur are actually deflated by his annotations, as when the eloquent nobility of *Grace M. Popich Symbolically Sketched*, with its sweeping staircase and flamboyant arch, is undercut by a circumstantial allusion to Rizzoli's annual open-house invitation to the Achilles Tectonic Exhibit (the A.T.E.): "In appreciation of the good taste she showed as she with a group of girl friends visited the A.T.E. during its second anniversary day being the first strangers to do so." Many of the interjections in the A.T.E. *Portfolio* itself are quite fatuous, as for instance the motto "Perpetual Virginity for Perpetual Youthfulness" (A.T.E. *Portfolio*, A–15); or this misguided attempt to mimic the adman: "You, too, will live in grand exposition style in patronizing the A.T.E. periodi-

cally" (A.T.E. *Portfolio*, A–2). One might also be inclined to groan at the punning supplementary title *Shirley's Temple* (alluding to the child movie star Shirley Temple, the very incarnation of cuteness) which Rizzoli cannot refrain from appending to *Shirley Jean Bersie Symbolically Sketched*. The supposed spiritual intensity of this image is further undermined by the sentimental note that records it was inspired by a visit when Shirley Bersie "rang the bell, sighing tenderly: 'Can I come in and see your pictures?'"

The general effect of Rizzoli's verbal interpolations is to augment the visual impact, introducing as it were a backup group to harmonize with and amplify the pictorial melody. At one moment Rizzoli exhibits the eloquence of the draftsman, confident in his technique; at the next, he becomes the over-zealous scribe who fears there is still a lot more to be said. At times he will expand on a given detail with an arrow and a fussy explanation; at others he will mark an elevation with story numbers and the functions of its rooms. In *The Ornament* (*Gigantic Symbolic Figure*), he slips in a small ground plan of *The Ornament* to indicate the disposition of some eighty door-high glass screens across the entire nave, and then elaborates on their ornate features in a pretentious and tiresome footnote. Elsewhere, he is so keen to show off his autodidact's knowledge that he makes a fool of himself, as when, in the A.T.E. *Portfolio* (sheet A–20), he adorns the architectural splendors of the Hotel Truregalhost with the silly recommendation, "A Book to Read 'Modern Architectural Design' by Howard Robertson companion volume to 'Architectural Composition.'" Other futile inserts celebrate obscure heroes from history: "Alfred Parsons, English Landscape Painter 1847–1920," "Matthew S. Quay, American politician and senator, 1833–1904," "Sir John Sandys, English classicist, 1844–1922" – all these from the same sheet of the A.C.E. *Bulletin* (sheet 325). Further adulterations of seriousness are effected by the impromptu labels, "A Bit of Architecture" or "A Bit of Heavenly Architecture," added to the buildings like the quips of some incompetent guide. Such habits reflect an unworldliness and want of tact in Rizzoli's curatorship of his own work.

A.C.E. 325. 1963. Graphite
on vellum, 24 x 36" (61 x
91.4 cm). Collection The
Ames Gallery, Berkeley

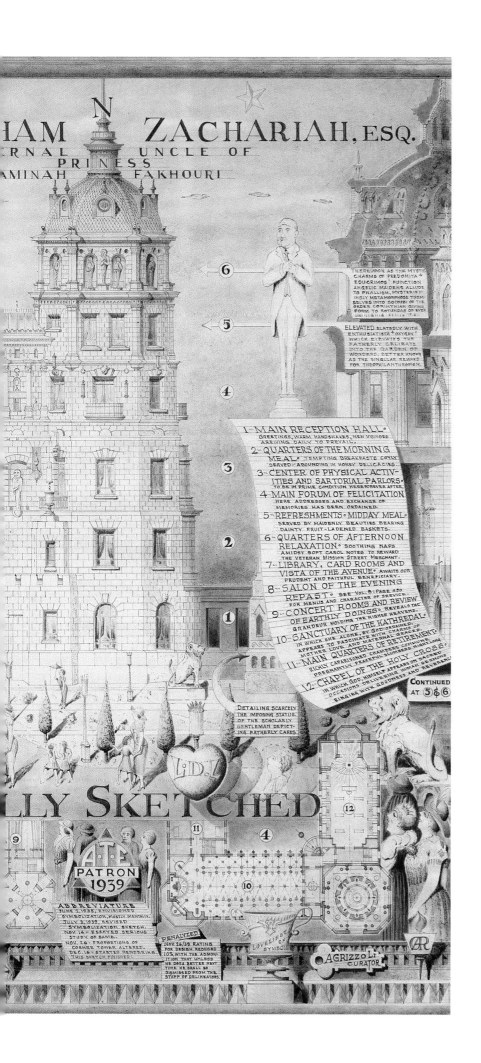

Abraham N. Zachariah
Symbolically Sketched/
Sanctuary del Uncle Abe.
1939. Ink on rag paper,
25⅝ x 35¾" (65.1 x 90.8
cm). Collection The Ames
Gallery, Berkeley

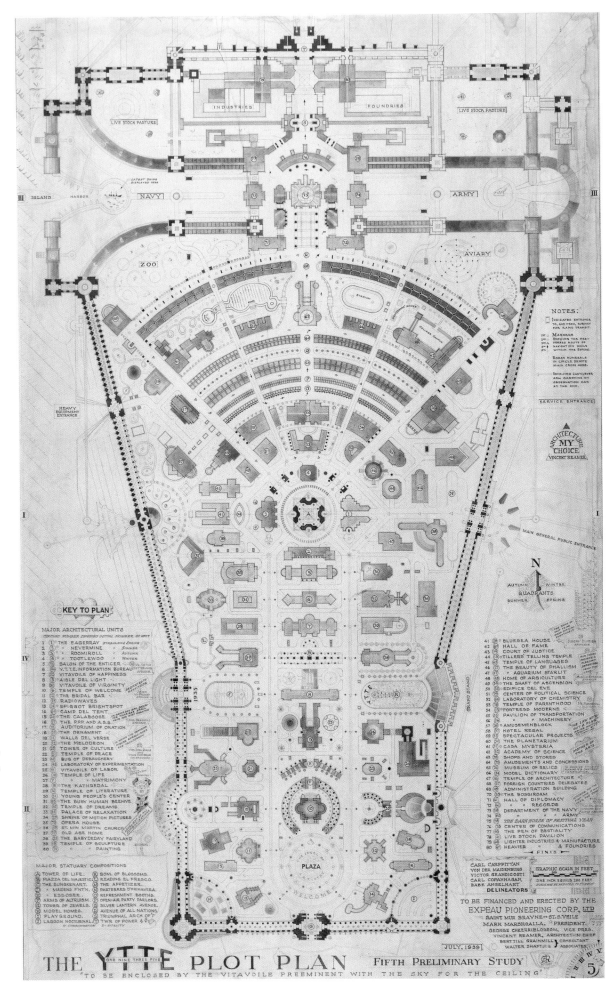

THE Y.T.T.E. PLOT PLAN —
FIFTH PRELIMINARY STUDY.
1939. INK ON RAG PAPER,
46 x 27¾" (116.8 x 70.5 CM).
COLLECTION THE AMES GALLERY,
BERKELEY

THE **YTTE** PLOT PLAN — FIFTH PRELIMINARY STUDY

Of the explicitly architectural drawings, the various Y.T.T.E. plot plans are laid out as convincing representations of Rizzoli's imaginary "Expeau" site. Invariably these plans bear numerals linked to an appended index of the eighty-odd units. The compelling symmetry of Rizzoli's layout and the sense of an intensely invested surface, taut with meanings, create a hypnotic effect. Of rather different impact is one drawing of the imaginary Isle del St Sans Vaile where the Y.T.T.E. is to be built. Credited to the delineator Babe Ilamme Angelhart, *The Place* is something of an aberration within the corpus. Comparatively free of verbal appendices, this representation of an uneven land mass embodies strange hachures that give it a more pictorial than diagrammatical look. (As if glued to an unreal sea, the island has something of the unsettling character of the ragged, nameless maps in some of Giorgio de Chirico's metaphysical paintings. It may also remind us of such fictive islands as Thomas More's Utopia, or Stevenson's Treasure Island. There may be a real-life link to the Treasure Island created in the San Francisco Bay for the 1939 Golden Gate Exhibition, though it is thought likely that the island shape derives from the reversed coastline of the southern tip of Marin County.) As a visual proposition, the image has a shaggy suggestiveness about it, even a hint of the obscene in that the two swollen promontories to the south of the "Proposed Site" of the Y.T.T.E. proper are tinted peach and look much like a penis and scrotum in profile.

This uncomfortable image stands in stark stylistic contrast to the clarity and abstemious control of the plot plans proper. It is as though here, in a uniquely macrocosmic overview of his utopia, Rizzoli had lost his grip on the safeguards of minutiae and been overtaken by an unaccustomed libidinal surge. Flouting normal routine, the eight encircled numerals scattered across the island are incorrectly referred to as 1 to 10 on an accompanying scroll, which blithely directs us outside the frame ("See official map for legend"). If it is a traditional courtesy of the cartographer to ensure no detail is incomplete, Rizzoli, normally so attentive, is here prepared to leave us in the lurch. Opening onto the unregulated prospect of the wild and the unpredictable, this piece begins to read like a blurted confession about the consequences of lifting repression.

Another unusual work, *Bluesea House,* may be seen as an extreme instance of the pictorial mode being overtaken by the verbal. (There are in fact several competing titles set within this one complex design.) Although there are indications of spatiality, the piece is so much overlaid with captions, asides, cartouches, and minute patternings that it flattens out into a pictographic chart. We may read it as a dazzling diagram of alternative propositions and directions interpolated within a geometric network of zooming arrows, speeding trackways, and light rays. Spangled with crowns, rosettes, buttons, wind roses, ribbons, and other paraphernalia, the whole thing is reminiscent of a celestial snakes-and-ladders board. Rizzoli's scheme purports to plot "the conversation and allied five points giving form,

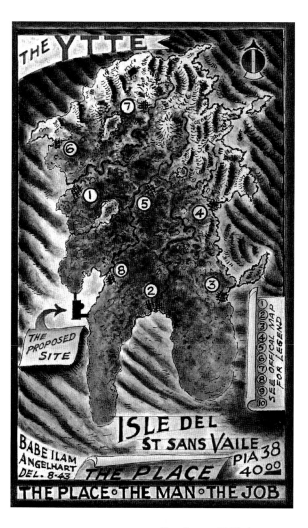

THE PLACE. 1943. INK ON RAG PAPER, 10 X 6" (25.4 X 15.2 CM). COLLECTION THE AMES GALLERY, BERKELEY

expression, and color to Joseph Bluesea's formula"; it is also intended to correspond to one of the units of the Y.T.T.E., Bluesea House. Its solemn captions in large capitals announce such slogans as "Charms of Maidenhood," while arrows converging on a five-point star sport the slogans "The Point of Greatest Good," "Defeating Virginity," "One Sweeping Penetration," "Life's Greatest Contention," "First in the Heart of God," and "The Start of New Life." The sobriety of the design's geometry is progressively adulterated by the sexuality of these verbal hints, especially those couched in tinier letters that necessitate the closer focus of the viewer's gaze and thus enforce an unexpected complicity: "Penetration intensity dynamically expressed as deducted by Mrs Quaile," "As orgasm approaches," or "Meaty manners of mating." A curious amalgam of cool geometry and raw sex seems designed to pinpoint those spatial and temporal coordinates where erotic feeling reaches its zenith; yet another caption speaks openly of "Phallism." Rizzoli's diagram is a fantasy guide to the erogenous zones, delineating the raptures of some atemporal and nonspatial utopia. There is even a droll touch of

science fiction in the technical notation: "This angle 90 degrees for finer results"; while the scale set along the bottom of the frame is captioned, "The slide rule of cooperation," as if to calibrate the exertions of coitus.

In at least one other crucial work, Rizzoli uses interpolated commentary to communicate a dimension of *phallism* that would otherwise have remained hidden behind a dispassionate architecture. The elevation of an improbably tall tower (in which one is tempted to see homage to the Coit Tower, erected in San Francisco two years earlier, though it is true that *Gerry George Gould Holt* resembled it more closely) sports this strange title in hefty swash capitals: *The Primalglimpse at Forty*, along with the subtitle *Interpreting the reactions experienced during that incomparable moment*. The moment referred to is pedantically recorded as having occurred between 2 and 4 on the afternoon of April 12, 1936, and represents an erotic epiphany in Rizzoli's life when, seemingly, he caught a glimpse of the bare body of a little girl at play. Rizzoli compresses a fund of associations onto a scroll affixed at top left, impersonally signed "The Delineators." Ascribing separate

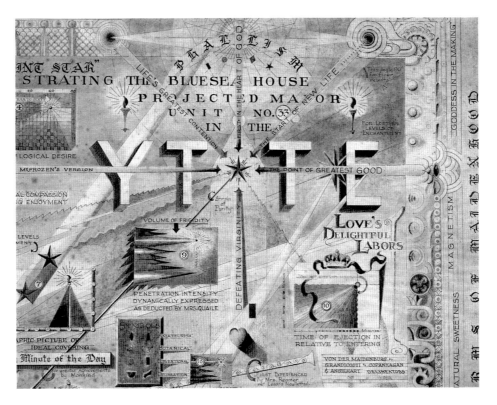

THE BLUESEA HOUSE (DETAIL). 1938. INK ON RAG PAPER, 20⅜ x 30⅜" (51.8 x 77.2 CM). COLLECTION MICHAEL GROSSMAN, NEW YORK

readings to the five "elevations" of the tower, it seems to imply the stages of a monumental erection. (By now we can hardly avoid imputing phallic meaning to Rizzoli's tapering skyscrapers.) There follows this further passage:

COMMENT: *Even in [sic] the face of substantiating coopera-tion on the part of the first party was lacking, being a tiny miss of three or so, playing unconcernedly on the ground in her backyard with her playmate, we now often wonder what amazing form of beauty or sense of originality could have resulted had there been timely, judiciously planned, more appropriately and properly stimulated cooperation on the part of the first party. Wondering, wondering, wondering we are engulfed in highly fascinating puzzling wonderment.*

The legend reflects a typical pattern of confession-and-evasion, in that the impulse to "tell all" is so strongly held in check by the counter-impulse to quell the revela-tion, or at least to stop its being blurted out too explicitly. A nuance of guiltiness comes across in the coy cliché of "a tiny miss," quickened by the phrase "amazing form of beauty." Yet these hints are wrapped around in highfalutin circumlocution and legalese. As a species of euphemism for the child, "the first party" seems to establish a con-tractual relationship. Yet, despite the pretentions of its rhetoric, the complaint about a lack of "timely, judiciously planned, more appropriately and properly stimulated co-operation" reeks of sheer sexual frustration. Here we may be inclined to censure the delineator; although it is true that, if we have divined the overriding revelation of his "primalglimse," we may also have entered into a form of complicity with him. The gist of this ambiguous textual performance is an appeal to our own sensations of won-derment, fascination, and puzzlement.

There is a further supplement. Onto the right-hand side of the same work, the artist pins yet another florid text, arranged in a triangle to balance a drawing of a cres-cent moon flanked by a barbin and a gargoyle. Also signed "The Delineators," it offers another defense and another sort of seduction. It reads thus:

APPRECIATION. *We sincerely believe we have delineated the most remarkable and singular impression ever possible of expressing in terms of decorative architecture unique to extremes hardly possible of visualization unless one has actually experienced the oddly intrinsic throbbing ordeal, thereupon we feel we have produced the most picturesque and precious piece of, or at least essayed the initial move in what may be considered a new movement in the history of art.*

Given the erotic context, the phrase "oddly intrinsic throbbing ordeal" can only be a circumlocution for *orgasm*, couched though it is with typical ambivalence insofar as "throbbing" is explicit, whereas "intrinsic" is so oblique as to be opaque.[5] More importantly, Rizzoli voices the strik-ing claim to have "essayed the initial move in what may be considered a new movement in the history of art." Now we may want to note the slogan along the top of the frame, "That you too may see something you've not seen before," and interpret it as a reference not so much to a male virgin's sexual epiphany as to what is in effect that same experience transmuted into "decorative architecture." Perhaps what Rizzoli is saying is that he has established a new artistic language for translating the secular into the sacred (invoking, as it were, the equivalence of two sorts of "erection"). This same language may also be operative in the vignettes at each top corner of the image, which show ornaments of Rizzoli's devising, the barbin and the gargoyle. Their respectively female and male connotations reflect the same reciprocity of the erotic and the architec-tural theme, while the notion of an equilibrium between sexuality and spirituality may be figured in the celestial balance that presides over *The Primalglimse* as a whole.

Having shown how Rizzoli as scribe tends to monitor, evaluate, and occasionally expose Rizzoli the draftsman, I would now like to examine the characteristics of his textual style and the odd nature of his relationship to language.

The indications are that Rizzoli's novel *The Colonnade* (from which he gives two choice extracts in the pages of the *A.T.E. Portfolio*) was thick with pretentious epithets and redundant periphrase. The repeated verse exercises that fill so many pages of the *A.C.E. Bulletin* in the 1960s are generally marked by maudlin repetition and slow-paced, often tortuous syntax. One finds tiresome, would-be-poetic distortions of syntax, along with frequent misspellings: *magnificiently, spectular, illuming*. Here is the first half of a poem dating from 1963–66 and bearing the bizarre title "Wright admitting fenestration."

New Year greetings, those outlasting snow
Are nigh, heart-warming, rapt'ring, sadd'ning few,
More enthralling, more art-walling, more
Ennobling than art-work in speckled blue.
Larger fenestration deem the cause,
The lilac reason why I'm here, aghast,
Seeing o'er vast spaces sent ship-like
Unknown before, transported joys surpassed.

Tidyings like these, tidal waves estranged
Have nothing, that are halved, in common, won,
Sung or swarfed outdoors, perplexing flairs
Incline inwardly, by faith-tithes outdone.
More sun burst, like fenestration in
The sky, by resurrection-thrusts' rose glow
Ventured, deem this year's "Good News" event –
Adventure making day of night half so.

(*A.C.E. Bulletin, sheet 325, page 688*)

A few intimations of sense surface here, despite the writer's infuriating obliquity and tone of coy circumspection. Rizzoli loves fine-sounding words, and "fenestration" is a beauty. It is of course also an architectural term, and the Wright invoked in the title turns out later in the text to be Frank Lloyd Wright; hence the reference to "larger fenestration" celebrates the fuller influx of light through windows in edifices. The poem seems to be saying that such architectural innovations are calculated to be more impressive than simple picture-making (though "art-work in speckled blue" remains obscure). This architectural discussion merges into a quasi religious vision in which the sky itself seems pierced by windows, releasing a "rose glow."

Despite Rizzoli's professed intention to use iambic pentameters, his stanzas stumble along with uneven stresses and paralyzed speech patterns that the liberal use of commas fails to relax. Internal rhymes, such as "enthralling / art-walling," arise with no attempt to justify their appropriateness to an overall message. The end rhymes are hardly inventive, though "aghast / surpassed" is a minor achievement. Contractions like "rapt'ring" and "sadd'ning" mimic outdated lyric diction. There are some idle sound contaminations: "tidyings," itself a gratuitous corruption of "tidings," prompts half-echoes in "tidal waves" and "faith-tithes," a way of skimming on the same syllable across different words with blithe disdain for semantic continuity. One line offers a flourish: "The lilac reason why I'm here, aghast," a catchy match of a color quality to an abstraction ("lilac reason") with an ironic shaft of self-deprecation ("aghast"), although this quasi modernistic effect is almost certainly fortuitous.

Such semiregulated babblings give off an air of purpose yet manifestly fail to achieve any sort of plain communication. The reader has the impression of an amnesiac who wants to say something yet keeps on losing the thread, and, in embarrassment, improvises without ever getting to the point, in a kind of linguistic strumming. Reading the text aloud several times over one senses that its author is not really behind what is being said: here is a species of vacuous ventriloquism, a speaking for the sake of speaking, an activity of irresponsible semiosis-without-referent. Rizzoli is wallowing in words rather than bending them to a meaning. The literary parallel is not so much the poetry of Dadaism – where incoherence thrives on an air of eventual meaning – as the freewheeling absurdity typical of the writings produced by mental patients with a reduced capacity to communicate.

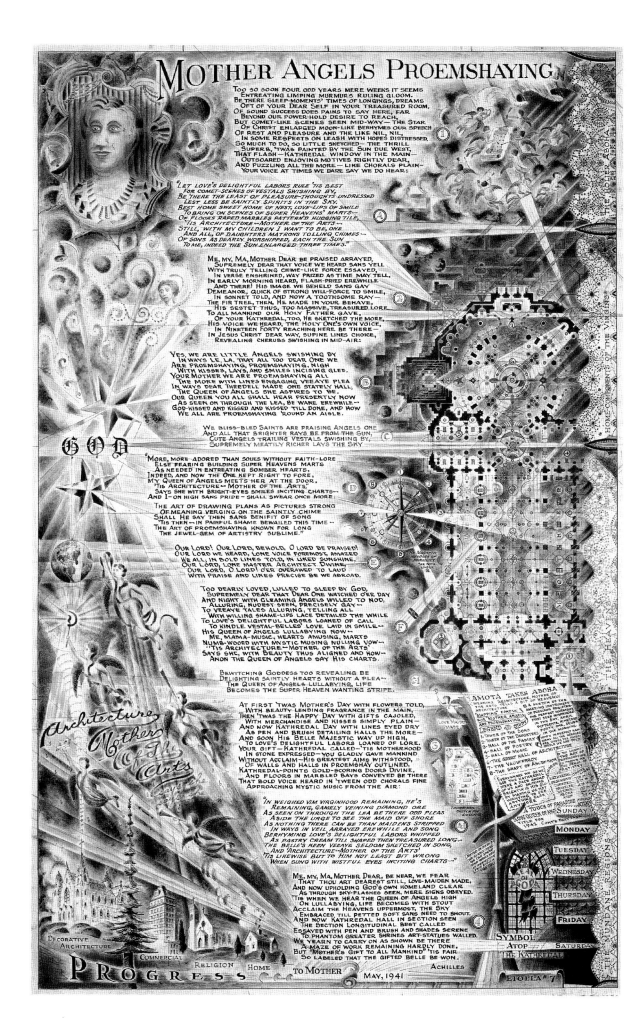

Mother Angels Proemshay-
ing. 1941. Ink on rag paper,
38 x 24" (96.5 x 61 cm).
Collection The Ames Gallery,
Berkeley

To press the point further, I would say that the broad sweep of Rizzoli's verbal production betrays a fundamental narcissism, since to make things sound impressive seems so much more important to him than to make any actual statement. Rizzoli has a self-seducing showman's approach to utterance. I can't but feel he is showing off to himself when he makes up those preposterous names for his various alter egos, collaborators, and sponsors: there is a shared falseness about such coinages as Peter Metermaid, Vincent Argent Reamer (an echo of "dreamer"?), John McFrozen, Fred Crossdegree, Babe Angelhart, Von der Maidenberg, Frank K. Delight, Mark Oxe Marshoalla, Berttill Grainmill, Mazelin Harbbor, Pearlned Opalleene, and Joseph Bluesea. While one may decipher "Virginia Gingerbred" as a playful allusion to a girl's ginger hair (along with puns on "gingerbread" and perhaps "thoroughbred"), there seems no point in dwelling on names like Thermae Joviallee, Belladora Blossomhart, and Leadda Maulettail (the maiden name of Mrs. Vincent Reamer), save to note an habitual and unnecessary doubling of consonants.

Once he takes verbal flight, Rizzoli displays a true passion for fanciful neologisms, as in such coinages as "proemshaying" (celebrating through poetry?), "ichnoraphy" and "orthoraphy" (modes of architectural projection), and the "vaulterroy" (an ornate altarpiece). However skeptical we may be of such novelties, we may occasionally find ourselves thrilling to absurdity, especially when the scribe expressly takes us into his secrets. A precious note in the *A.C.E. Bulletin* (sheet 301, page 591D) discloses that "the Eagerray," "the Nevermine," "the Roomiroll," and "the Tootlewoo" – all buildings identified on the Y.T.T.E. plan – are poetic names for, respectively, the Courts of Spring, Summer, Autumn, and Winter. Another note in the *A.T.E. Portfolio* confides that "Sayanpeau" was a sound-word spontaneously voiced by the three-and-a-half-year-old Irwin Sicotte in an attempt to communicate the idea "Wait a moment!" (*A.T.E. Portfolio*, sheet A–10): the fact that no reader could possibly have guessed this demonstrates just how important it was for Rizzoli to possess secrets, to share or not share at will. When he takes the trouble to inform us that the word "sympa" means "a portfolio featuring all four elements" (*A.T.E. Portfolio*, sheet A–9), we sense his pride in his own arcane invention, pointless though it may seem to us. Another sheet of the *Portfolio* sees Rizzoli putting forward the neologism "piafore." With hair-raising whimsicality, he announces that whereas he was "probably influenced by the word 'pinafore' meaning a small apron won [sic] by children or little girls" (*A.T.E. Portfolio*, sheet A–2), he is intent henceforth upon using "piafore," or rather its abbreviation "pia," to designate a "message lettered without adornments" (*A.T.E. Portfolio*, sheet A–16), that is: a simplified, small-size, low-priced copy of an item from the Y.T.T.E. list. (Such copies were assigned an individual "Pia" number in Rizzoli's inventory.) The reader who has absorbed this information will smile to find a disingenuous note on a separate page of the same portfolio which claims that "We shall deem it a [sic] honor to see some learned linguist derive a sensible and concise definition for piafore which seems to be beyond our power to do so" (*A.T.E. Portfolio*, sheet A–4.)

Weird indeed is the associative impulse that prompts the writer, as happens in another context, to switch over from the familiar Latin word *"novena"* (a Catholic devotion) to the unfamiliar *novella,* found in the dictionary: "refreshing on the meaning of 'novena,' preceding this word by a couple of words, in Webster's International will be found 'novella'."[4] While he is scrupulous enough to cite the true meaning of this last (an Italian term referring to a romance narrative), we next witness Rizzoli categorically giving himself carte blanche to adapt it to his own ends, contending with utter assurance – and not a little opacity – that "whether or not the word is appropriate, its novelty and its affinity and cementitious qualities has [sic] affixed itself to call 'novella' the so-called 'elephant size' versification-aspect comprising verses, auxiliary comment, graphic delineation, intercession, chronology, et cetera" (*A.C.E. Bulletin*, sheet 381, page 829B). In other words, Rizzoli is following Humpty Dumpty's magisterial principle of making a word mean anything he chooses it to mean.

One might see such willful, perhaps even ponderous, tamperings with the shape and standard meaning of words as symptomatic of a quasi autistic desire to hijack normal parlance and head out for horizons beyond the jurisdiction of the dictionary. Once such delirious appropriations are legitimized, each caprice acquires talismanic potency as a sound-cluster, on a par with a magic word like *abracadabra*. Rizzoli surely felt the power of nonsense and opacity, and only occasionally took pleasure in piously explaining his anarchic methods.

A passion for acronyms is surely the key symptom of Rizzoli's verbal addiction, and may be said to service two levels of communication. To transpose the name of a given project or organization into an acronym can establish a useful shorthand for participants in that enterprise, as well as confirming their identity with that terse label. Rizzoli's acronyms seem to reflect a hankering to be part of a complicitous circle; yet just as Rizzoli's architectural team is largely chimerical, so the acronyms he invokes take on the character of a dismissal or a challenge to those not in on the game. As long as its encoder is the sole person in the know, a code's only function is to embody his authority: the code has to be explicated at some point if other people are to be drawn into the circle of understanding.

A glimpse into Rizzoli's mystificatory routines can be gained from looking at sheet 301 of the *A.C.E. Bulletin* (comprising pages 591A–594B). These eight pages, prepared during the early 1960s, include yet another rendering of the Y.T.T.E. plot plan, along with related poems whose grand-sounding (and slightly scatty) titles secrete acronymic references to familiar words or initials: "Admirably Grandest Relationship" (AGR), "Amte Betty Carillon" (ABC), "Labor's Anniversary Day" (LAD), and "Preller's Animation Dioramic" (PAD). A bizarre "Auxiliary Comment" is added which, having gnomically recommended that the reader seek meaning "by reading, in the dark, the poem and looking, in bright sunlight, at its pictorial companion," goes on to announce that "Y.T.T.E." should be pronounced "It-Tea," and that it is "Betty's uncorrupted project." (However, we might note an inconsistency on this point, since in another context "Y.T.T.E." is spelled out as "Why

tea-tee eee": see *The Nevermine*, 1944.) Other evidence indicates that the same acronym came to signify "Yield to Total Elation," though the "Auxiliary Comment" could be hinting that it originally derived from the reversed letters of part of the name *Betty*. A few sheets further on in the *Bulletin*, Rizzoli yields a further obscure clue in the form of a message inserted into five circles alongside the poem "Electrifying TYTTE Candidates" of 1961–63, which reads: "The YTTE? Betty's Tytte Project" (*A.C.E. Bulletin* sheet 304, page 599B). But how much has Rizzoli really told us? Should we discern a pun here on "tight," or on "titty"? Was there a real person named Betty Tytte? It would seem that the same female friend and muse – she had earned Rizzoli's pious affection as a result of her support during his open-house events in the late 1930s – was also dubbed "Amte Betty Carillon," and subsequently rechristened "Rechi Tacteur" or "Rechi Amte Tacteur." The tantalizing nickname A.M.T.E. is known to secrete (or to generate) the slogan "Architecture Made To Entertain," while the oft-repeated formula "A.C.E." signifies "AMTE's Celestial Extravaganza," an instance of two layers of compressed meaning.

A way of compounding the disguise is to transcribe the acronym as a proper noun. Thus "ESSOSEE" is a rewriting of "S.O.C." or the "Spirit of Cooperation," while "VEEAYE" comes from "V.A.E." – the initials of Virginia Ann Entwistle. Rizzoli's daft habit of cramming associations within brief mottoes crystallizes in the phrase "AMOTA takes ABOHA" (the title of a scroll inset within *Mother Angels Proemshaying*). This is exuberantly decoded as "Architecture Mother of the Arts tells [sic] a Bit of Heavenly Architecture." Such examples show how malleable the acronym could be in Rizzoli's hands, a device to compress existing meanings and to conjure up new ones.

The transparent derivation of the name "Rechi Tacteur" from "Architecture" might prompt us to try to detect anagrams in Rizzoli's texts. Unfortunately, the search proves to be somewhat futile, since, without clear signals of intent, it is rarely possible to be sure whether one has indeed identified a true anagram. Thus one might speculate that A.M.T.E. comes from *team* or *mate* – but, then, might it not also be a near-anagram of *emma*, the name of Rizzoli's mother, or perhaps of the surname of Virginia Tamke? Again, the similar oddity *sarmte* could come from *master* (if not from *stream*): such surmising doesn't really take us very far. What can be said with confidence is that these riddles, however constructed, are important to Rizzoli insofar as they trigger acronymic meanings, as when "S.A.R.M.T.E." opens up onto "Symbolic Architectural Romance Taught to Entertain" (an embellishment of "A.M.T.E." in the sense of "Architecture Made to Entertain"). It is always to the acronym that Rizzoli returns, as to a favorite trick for fertilizing the imagination.

One of Rizzoli's few attempts to invent a genuine cipher is found in a scrolled statement smuggled into the top corner of *Janet M. Peck Painted Pictorially*, which reads, all in capital letters: "Ju ublft pme spnbo cmppe up jotujuvuf uif fyrvjtjuf." The code is easily broken once one realizes that each letter has been shifted one stage on in the alphabet, and that, shifted back, the phrase reads: "It takes old Roman blood to institute the exquisite." The naiveté of this subterfuge is compounded by the paltriness of the secret we uncover, and hastens the thought that few of Rizzoli's verbal puzzles can be so deep that it is worth wrestling with them for very long.

The fact that I have on occasion found Rizzoli vexing by no means implies that I dismiss his achievement at large. I see two things to be indisputably impressive about his work. One is the meticulousness with which, in the early pictures and plans, he went about visualizing and annotating a project he must have known could never materialize. The other is the sheer obduracy with which, across two decades, he added page upon page to the A.C.E. *Bulletin*, that unfinishable dossier of inspirations which only death would close. We have seen that, much like other Outsider mythographers, Rizzoli revels in the narcissistic thrill of absolute imaginative potency, whether savoring the prospects of a skyscraping *phallism* or constructing abstruse

textual defenses that keep the outside world at bay. Yet unless we assume that a supreme schizoid conviction can totally override actual circumstance, we would do well to remember that Rizzoli died both an undiscovered autodidact and a sexual failure. As so often happens in the context of Outsiderdom, our final assessment of a splendid creative endeavor may not be easy to disentangle from our knowledge of an existential sacrifice. "Now there's no more any longer any reason for feeling lonely" is the announcement on the cover of the A.T.E. *Portfolio*: clumsily strung out, the maxim has a callow gaiety that betrays its hollowness.

Let me close by pointing to Rizzoli's own rare admission of the humble truth. It is a 1940 drawing in the A.T.E. *Portfolio* (sheet A–13) depicting the "Home of the A.T.E." – the modest dwelling on Alabama Street where the man lived for most of his life, and the venue of his hopeful annual shows. In stark contrast to the lofty elevations he usually drafts, this realistic three-quarter view shows a single-story cottage with wooden steps: Rizzoli even dubs it "The Shanty." A floor plan of the interior and the backyard situates for us such pathetic features as "Mother's Bed" (she had been dead for three years by now), "Sister's Phonograph," "Ironing Board," "Inclined Driveway to Garage," "Clothes Line," and "Chestnut Tree." Alongside, Rizzoli sets out a diagram showing the disposition on the four walls of the front room where the Achilles Tectonic Exhibit was held. Having so often witnessed him trumpeting the miracles of symbolic transfiguration, we may suppose that, for once, Rizzoli felt obliged to register the utter banality of his literal life. Deep down, the mighty Achilles avowed the true identity of "Il Piccolino" – the Little 'Un. Indeed, a rueful note dating from 1966 admits that "graphic delineation" requires "the sacrifice of being in the mood, a form of living with one foot on earth, the other in heaven, that is, stretching the imagination to the breaking point – a practice not recommended while payment of bills is pending" (A.C.E. *Bulletin* sheet 381, page 829B). Uplifted by spiritual and erotic visions, and disguised by pseudonyms and neologisms, Rizzoli could claim the status of Celestial Architect; all the same, as recluse and celibate scribbler, he remained earthbound in the suburban anonymity of San Francisco's Bernal Heights.

NOTES

1. Kay Redfield Jamison, *Touched with Fire: Manic-Depressive Illness and the Artistic Temperament* (New York: The Free Press, 1993), 122.

2. John MacGregor, "I See a World Within the World: I Dream but Am Awake," in *Parallel Visions: Modern Artists and Outsider Art*, ed. Maurice Tuchman (Los Angeles: Los Angeles County Museum of Art, in conjunction with Princeton University Press, 1992), 247.

3. Sander L. Gilman, "Constructing Creativity and Madness: Freud and the Shaping of the Psychopathology of Art," in Tuchman, 233.

4. A. G. Rizzoli, A.C.E. 407, Auxiliary comment 855–C, 17 March 1966. Henceforth, all A.C.E. citations are direct quotes from Rizzoli's writings.

5. My warmest thanks to Bonnie Grossman, director of The Ames Gallery, Berkeley, California, who conducted much of the early research on Rizzoli, and who graciously shared her findings with me through interviews on numerous occasions between 1990 and 1996.

6. The *Festival Year* referred to the Panama-Pacific International Exposition held in San Francisco in 1915.

7. Rizzoli makes periodic references to this throughout the A.C.E. and the A.T.E. *Portfolio*, mostly self-congratulatory for his asceticism, which he believed to be crucial for having spiritual experiences. Rizzoli also created drawings such as the *Vitavoile of Virginity* as early as 1940, aka *Fountain of the Maidens*, and later a shrine, known as the VASP (Virginity – A Shrine Potential) or VOW (Virginity's Odd Wonders), to commend his efforts in this area.

8. Lists of library books were found among his effects, evidence of a prodigious reader with complex and varied interests, including submarine engineering, photography, civics, financial investments, architecture, marriage and sex, watch repair, and ordnance and explosives. The many how-to books on Rizzoli's lists reveal his desire to join the booming economy of the 1920s, as do his later attempts to "make money at home" with his writings and drawings. Rizzoli, "Books" list, 1919–22. Unpublished papers, The Ames Gallery.

9. His papers also included lists of other potential devices that he considered producing, including a "Self-Running Toy" (1917), an "Instrument for Drawing Ellipses" (1918), an "Automatic Signal Bell for Highways" (1921), and "Air Balloons in the Form of Birds – Animals, etc." (1921). Rizzoli, "Possible Inventions," 1917–21. Unpublished papers, The Ames Gallery.

10. Rizzoli, unpublished papers, The Ames Gallery.

11. Rizzoli, letter to Bank of America, 2 October 1933. The Ames Gallery.

12. Rizzoli, Individual Income Tax Return for 1928. The Ames Gallery.

13. One of these letters, from an editor that he paid to review his work, described his efforts as "twenty thousand words without a story." Laurence R. D'Orsay to Rizzoli, 28 January 1927, 2. Unpublished papers, The Ames Gallery.

14. Rizzoli, *Colonnaded Plaza*. Unpublished manuscript, 1927, 7. The Ames Gallery.

15. A.C.E. 342, Poem 879–3–0, 29 November 1964.

16. A.C.E. 337, Auxiliary comment 752–B, 11 November 1963.

17. So known because of their inception and principal advocacy at the Ecole

OVERLEAF: **WALLS DEL VERSE** (DETAIL). 1937

des Beaux-Arts in Paris, from the late 18th century until the time of the Second World War. The Beaux-Arts' ideas about architecture and methods of instruction became the first formal model for architectural training in the United States during the early years of this century; it was not until after the Depression that modernist idioms began making significant inroads into this then-conservative profession.

18. Rizzoli's use of light rays is a recurring idiom in his work. Beyond the obvious connection to spectacular secular events, they also recall the auras emanating from heroic or heavenly figures found throughout art history that indicate divine grace or genius, and they reference heavenly visions and dialogue with God. Rizzoli specifically mentioned rays of light as part of the visions he experienced, and interpreted them in the same way.

19. Kevin Michael Day astutely noted Rizzoli's innovative juxtapositions of distinct iconographic elements: "Rizzoli's drawings present an ingenious interface between the high art of the Beaux-Arts rendering, and the popular mode of the commercial advertisement. Unlike the more democratic perspectives proposed by current social theories of art, the hierarchical division between the high and the popular was the accepted convention in the 1930s. This fact makes Rizzoli's art all the more unique from our present understanding." Day, "Allegorical Architecture: Interpreting the Visions of A.G. Rizzoli" thesis (Master's thesis, University of California at Berkeley, 1995), 26.

20. The architectural Eclecticism movement, popularized in the United States from 1880 through the 1930s, attempted to combine disparate styles under a unifying rubric. The goal of these buildings was to reduce elements to their essentials: balance, simplicity, and refinement. Although Rizzoli's drawings bring together a variety of architectural styles in one form, they widely miss the marks of unity and simplicity; if anything, the viewer is simultaneously distracted and attracted by the visual overload of the individual elements, rather than compelled by a harmonious whole. For additional information on the Eclecticism movement in relation to Rizzoli's work, see Day, 31 ff.

21. Rizzoli, *The Y.T.T.E. Plot Plan, Fourth Preliminary Study,* 1938.

22. Several of Rizzoli's renderings for Deichmann's firm were found among his effects. Deichmann's designs were rather unimaginative, and these renderings differ markedly from the drawings Rizzoli did on his own time: there is little ornamentation, no creative fusion of disparate elements, and an inclination toward modernist versus classical styling.

23. Margaret E. Griffin, coworker in Deichmann's firm 1937–38, interview with Bonnie Grossman and John MacGregor, 18 June 1991.

24. Rizzoli rarely referred to his father in all of his voluminous writings and drawings. By contrast, Deichmann's death inspired a significant number of poems, portraits, and sketches for his "heavenly inheritance," evidence of the importance he must have held for his young employee; even Deichmann's mother was honored with a major Symbolization drawing.

25. *A.C.E.* 517, Auxiliary comment 862–W, 8 November 1972.

26. "Rather than bluntly saying 'I love you, Mother' the theory here is to convey the identical meaning in terms of an edifice of ecclesiastical grandeur . . . ." *A.C.E.* 517, 862–Z, n.d. [c. 8 November 1972].

27. Rizzoli also made Christmas cards for his mother, which he addressed and stamped, mailing them to the house in which he lived, for some twenty years after her death. Gary Grauberger, Rizzoli's grand-nephew, telephone interview with author, 1 March 1996.

28. Gary Grauberger, telephone interview with author 1 March 1996. Mr. Grauberger and his family had cleared out Rizzoli's home after his stroke.

29. *A.C.E.* 492, Auxiliary comment 889–C, 29 July 1970.

30. Margaret E. Griffin, interview with Bonnie Grossman and John MacGregor, 18 June 1991.

31. *A.C.E.* 308, Chronological comment 616, 22 February 1962.

32. Donna and Marty D'India, former neighbors, interview with Bonnie Grossman and John MacGregor, 2 September 1991.

33. *A.C.E.* 373, 823–R, 22 August 1965.

34. *A.C.E.* 492, Auxiliary comment 889–E, 19 August 1970.

35. Day, 2–3.

36. Michael Schuyt, Joost Elffers, and George R. Collins, *Fantastic Architecture: Personal and Eccentric Visions* (New York: Harry N. Abrams, 1980), 9.

37. Lewis Mumford, *Sticks and Stones: A Study of American Architecture and Civilization* (New York: Dover Publications, 1955), 193.

38. Ibid., 197.

39. The Y.T.T.E. was inspired by Reamer's revelation that he preferred colonnades to "maids," noted in Rizzoli's 1927 manuscript. "Upon uttering these . . . simple words, . . . Vincent [saw] the light of a new era which

first took root in the Colonnade and which after ten odd years blossomed out vividly into the glorious, all-amazing Y.T.T.E." *A.T.E. Portfolio*, 1940, A–4.

40. Grossman has hypothesized that Reamer, "father" of the Y.T.T.E., may also have been an alter-ego of A. G.'s own father. She bases this on the seeming similarity between the names Innocente and Vincent, and on the connotations of Reamer's name (Vincent=Winner, Argent= Silver, Reame=Kingdom) referencing triumphal ascension to the heavenly Y.T.T.E. region. Reamer actually seems to combine attributes of both men.

41. *A.T.E. Portfolio*, 1940, A–10.

42. Gary Grauberger, telephone interview with author, 1 March 1996.

43. *A.T.E. Portfolio*, 1940, A–19.

44. *A.T.E. Portfolio*, 1940, A–4.

45. *A.C.E.* 355, Auxiliary comment 804–B, 21 December 1964.

46. *A.C.E.* 316, Comment 647–B, 12 August 1962.

47. *A.C.E.* 455, Auxiliary comment 251–S, 25 March 1969.

48. *A.C.E.* 349, Comments, Developments, Etc., 779–B, 5 June 1964.

49. *A.C.E.* 328, Auxiliary comment 710–C, n.d. [May 1963].

50. In Tuchman, 256.

51. The equal significance afforded every structure suggests comparisons with numerous environmental assemblages constructed in an additive mode, so that as each component is created, it becomes an indispensable and equivalently valued part of the whole.

52. In Tuchman, 273.

53. *A.C.E.* 489, Auxiliary comment 850–O, P, 5 July 1966.

54. *A.C.E.* 345, 774–D, n.d. [March 1964].

55. Although certainly some of the structures Rizzoli created – such as the cathedral – are part of our common heritage, most of them are invented.

Some of his buildings fulfill purposes as intriguing as their names.

56. Rizzoli's disinclination to readily divulge the meaning of his invented words is in marked contrast to his readiness to clarify both the meaning and pronunciation of standard words that he felt might not have widespread usage.

57. *A.C.E.* 443, Auxiliary comment 858–L, 27 August 1967.

58. *A.C.E.* 359, Supplementary 809–G, 27 September 1964.

59. *A.C.E.* 479, Implementing 806–2–K, 9 January 1970.

60. Later also referred to as the Acme of Christian Exaltation and the Acme of Christian Endeavor (*A.C.E.* 398, Auxiliary Comment 844–E, 3 June 1966), and Animated Christian Endeavor. *A.C.E.* 408, Memoranda 856–D, 15 August 1966.

61. Later definitions of this acronym include Architecture Moored to Entertain and Architecture Manned to Entertain.

62. *A.C.E.* 210, "Introduction to CAPS Series," section B, n.d.

63. It may be assumed that Rizzoli had no preconception that the *A.C.E.* would become as massive as it did; periodically (after poems 96, 192, 800, and others) he writes of finishing, although he continued until his health prohibited further work almost twenty years after *A.C.E.*'s inception.

64. As the *A.C.E.* developed, Rizzoli distinguished less and less between biblical figures, historical eminences, saints, and neighbors.

65. *A.C.E.* 212, Poem 30, 21 March 1958.

66. *A.C.E.* 381, Supplement 829–B, 16 January 1966.

67. *A.C.E.* 416, Auxiliary comment 862–D, 8 October 1969. In the 1939 *Kathredal* drawing are references to "Mother's love of poetry, paintings and music."

68. *A.C.E.* 446, Auxiliary comment 877–F, 23 October 1967.

69. Examples include "The Wonder Worker" or "The Sonneteer" for St. Anthony; "John the Decorated" for John Fitzgerald Kennedy; and "Jesus' Prioress" for Miss Amte.

70. *A.C.E.* 413, Auxiliary comment 858–E, 27 October 1966.

71. *A.C.E.* 363, CARE 7, 7 March 1965.

72. *A.C.E.* 363, CARE section 2, 14 February 1965. The *A.C.E.* does include one sheet of typed poems, copied from those hand lettered in December 1959–January 1960. The typed versions are not illustrated, nor do they include Rizzoli's usual annotations on the meter used, when the verse was initially composed, lettered, and reviewed, the lists of those responsible for "collaborating" on the poem, biblical references, and so on. Without all this, as well as the distinctiveness added by his hand lettering and accompanying illustrations, the typed pages are much less imposing.

73. The book list from 1921 included *Making Advertisements and Making Them Pay* and *Typography of Advertisements That Pay*, resources upon which he undoubtedly drew in designing and attempting to market his *A.C.E.* works.

74. *A.C.E.* 351, Title page, n.d.

75. *A.C.E.* 399, Auxiliary comment 827–I, 14 June 1966.

76. *A.C.E.* 363, CARE section 5, 21 February 1965.

77. *A.C.E.* 329, Auxiliary comment 713–E, n.d. [June 1963].

78. *A.C.E.* 338, Auxiliary comment 754–B, n.d. [November 1963].

79. *A.C.E.* 338, Auxiliary comment 754–C, July 13, 1962 (In fact, Rizzoli dated this page incorrectly; it was actually 1964.)

80. Rizzoli's inclinations in both areas led him to philosophize about their

linkages with a metaphor of two branches sprouting from a "mysterious, mystic flowering shrub." (*A.C.E.* 225, "The CAPS Series – Explanatory Remarks," 1, 9 February 1959.) He was not alone in this theory. It should not be surprising that artists – particularly those who are self-taught – often combine the two, for such juxtapositions are found throughout the daily stream of information that our world produces through advertising, comics, television, and so forth. Although the fashion to follow suit comes and goes in the world of "high" art, Paul Klee spoke for many when he affirmed that "the act of writing and the act of representing are at bottom one and the same thing." Michel Thevoz, *Art Brut* (New York: Rizzoli International Publications, 1976), 104.

81. Wölfli, too, signed "every paragraph of his narrative, be it as Adolf Wölfli, or as Doufi, or as St. Adolf II. In addition, he complements his names by various attributes or substitutes such attributes for his names." Elsbeth Pulver, "Signed: Adolf Wölfli, a Victim of Misfortune. Language Structure in Adolf Wölfli's Written Work," in *Adolf Wölfli*, eds. Elka Spoerri and Jürgen Glaesemer (Berne: The Adolf Wölfli Foundation, Museum of Fine Arts, 1976), 68.

82. See A. G. Rizzoli's Self-Referential Titles for a fuller listing of names.

83. *A.C.E.* 363, CARE section 8, 7 March 1965.

84. *A.C.E.* 421, CARE 10, n.d.

85. *A.C.E.* 363, CARE 3, 14 February 1965. Sheet 500 of the *A.C.E.* included a catalogue of his "novellei," noting which parts were of interest to different audiences. Of the 63 that he notated, Rizzoli described 17 to be of "general interest," 8 of "family inter-

est," 26 of "Catholic faith interest," and 11 of "limited interest." Among the latter were those whose subject was the Y.T.T.E.

86. *A.C.E.* 380, Supplement 828–F, 21 November 1965.

87. *A.C.E.* 208, Poem 3, 15 February 1958.

88. Note the acronym PIA formed from this title, a reference to one of the earlier SYMPA categories of works.

89. Rizzoli manifested a real love of chess, even sketching out examples of game strategies complete with the "Rizzolian move." However, he indicated that his employer and a great-grand-nephew were the only people he ever played with, for usually he played "solitaire" against himself. *A.C.E.* 503, Auxiliary comment 778–2–C, n.d. [25 August 1972]. His niece recalled that no chess board had been found among his effects, and postulated that he had played these solitary games only on paper. Evelyn Codoni Grauberger, interview with Bonnie Grossman and John MacGregor, 12 February 1991.

90. *A.C.E.* 513 includes a very sketchy list of "Contemplated Projects," which include such topics as electricity, whiskers, snow, tall men, and so on. The title of this sheet is "Ad Astra – To the Stars." n.d.

91. *A.C.E.* 362, Supplement 817–C, 22 November 1964.

92. *A.C.E.* 336, Auxiliary comment 744–B, n.d. [September 1963].

93. *A.C.E.* 363, "Comment, Analysis, Retrospection, Etc. (CARE)," section 1, February 1965.

94. Thevoz, 48.

95. *A.C.E.* 488, Auxiliary comment 882–G, 2 April 1970.

96. *A.C.E.* 372, Auxiliary comment 823–K, n.d. [August 1965].

97. *A.C.E.* 364, CARE paragraph 12, 21 March 1965.

98. *A.C.E.* 511, Auxiliary comment 893–F, 3–4 August 1972.

99. *A.C.E.* 402, Auxiliary comment 850–D, 5 July 1966.

100. *A.C.E.* 378, Plot Plan Development 819–Z, n.d. [November–December 1965].

101. *A.C.E.* 499, Auxiliary comment 875–K, n.d. [19 May 1971].

102. *A.C.E.* 454, "Molten E. Allegheny" 251–M, n.d. [May 1968].

103. Walter Morgenthaler, M.D. *Madness and Art: The Life and Works of Adolf Wölfli* (Lincoln: The University of Nebraska Press, 1992), 90.

104. *A.C.E.* 375, Supplement 819–N, 3 October 1965.

105. *A.C.E.* 348, Page 778–H, 23 January 1970.

106. *A.C.E.* 338, Auxiliary comment 754–C, 13 July 1962. (See footnote 79 for clarification.)

107. *A.C.E.* 456, Auxiliary comment 251–V, 7 June 1968.

108. Theodor Spoerri, "Identity of Representation and the Represented in the Art of Adolf Wölfli," in Spoerri and Glaesemer, 94.

109. Although he periodically complained about the trouble he experienced translating his visions onto paper, he was even more daunted when he attempted a drawing from life of St. Anthony's Church: "sketching directly opposite, but from a point a block away, resulted in an experience both persuasive and embarrassing in that the magnitude of the project (versus spiritual communing) was both time-consuming and an exceptional novelty . . . . Unfortunately without the aid of photographs or surveyor's instruments, proportions were obtained by eye only, using the artist's method of holding the pencil at arm's length and comparing proportions of major elements with one

another." *A.C.E.* 507, Auxiliary comment 891–c, 891–g, 11 April 1972.

110. *A.C.E.* 437, Auxiliary comment 872–E, 23 June 1967.

111. *A.C.E.* 296, Prose narration for Poem 581, 2, 3 July 1961.

112. *A.C.E.* 502, Auxiliary comment 848–P, 17 July 1972.

113. *A.C.E.* 427, Auxiliary comment 866–H, 1 June 1967.

114. *A.C.E.* 373, Page 823–s, 22 August 1965.

115. *A.C.E.* 380, Supplement 828–B, 17 November 1965.

116. Rizzoli's "novellei" were *A.C.E.* sheets that were assigned the same number and tied together by theme, in contrast to the common definition of this term.

117. *A.C.E.* 529, Auxiliary comment 900–I, 13 February 1976.

118. Rizzoli, *Mr. O. A. Deichmann's Mother – Toure D'Longevity*, 1938.

119. Rizzoli, *Brother Lou and Sister Palmira Lievre Symbolically Sketched*, 1941.

120. *A.C.E.* 443, Auxiliary comment 858–M, n.d. [27 August 1967].

121. Everett P. Dulit, M.D., Clinical Associate Professor of Psychiatry, Albert Einstein College of Medicine, letter to Bonnie Grossman, 11 June 1996.

BEARDSLEY: THE JOY ZONE

1. Quotations from Gerry Holt are taken from an interview, March 1996.

2. For more on Beaux-Arts education, see Richard Chafee, "The Teaching of Architecture at the Ecole des Beaux-Arts," in *The Architecture of the Ecole des Beaux-Arts,* ed. Arthur Drexler (New York: Museum of Modern Art, 1977), 61–110.

3. For a close study of a *Prix de Rome* competition, see Neil Levine, "The Competition for the *Grand Prix* in 1824: a Case Study in Architectural Education at the Ecole des Beaux-Arts," in *The Beaux-Arts and Nineteenth-Century French Architecture*, ed. Robin Middleton (Cambridge: M.I.T. Press, 1982), 67–123.

4. We have confirmation of the importance of Banister Fletcher's book to Rizzoli from Gerry Holt, who received a copy of the 1938 edition as a Christmas gift from Rizzoli in 1941. The possibility that the illustrations in Fletcher's book might have influenced Rizzoli to add notations to his drawings was first proposed in an unpublished Master's thesis by Kevin Day, "Allegorical Architecture: Interpreting the Visions of A. G. Rizzoli" (Master's thesis, University of California at Berkeley, 1995), 23. There are other areas in which Kevin Day's analysis of Rizzoli's work anticipates mine, especially in his recognition of the importance of ideas about narrative architecture. I am most grateful to him to making a copy of his thesis available to me.

5. On the sources of inspiration for the Panama-Pacific Exposition, see John D. Barry, *The City of Domes* (San Francisco: John J. Newbegin, 1915); for more on Maybeck's Palace of Fine Arts and its sources, see Sally B. Woodbridge, *Bernard Maybeck: Visionary Architect* (New York: Abbeville Press, 1992), 98–111.

6. For a recent study of the architecture of the Panama-Pacific Exposition, see Gray Brechin, "Sailing to Byzantium: The Architecture of the Fair," in *The Anthropology of World's Fairs*, ed. Burton Benedict (Berkeley: Scolar Press, 1983), 94–113.

7. For an analysis of the ideology and aesthetics of the City Beautiful Movement, see William Wilson, *The City Beautiful Movement* (Baltimore: Johns Hopkins University Press, 1989). Quotations are from pp. 92–93.

8. On the place of commerce in City Beautiful schemes, see Daniel Bluestone, *Constructing Chicago* (New Haven: Yale University Press, 1991), 194–98.

9. The "messages" transmitted in the architecture of the exposition are examined in George Starr, "Truth Unveiled: The Panama-Pacific International Exposition and its Interpreters," in Benedict, *World's Fairs*, 134–75. Quotes are from pp. 138, 143.

10. John Barry's observations on the Joy Zone are from *The City of Domes*, 36. Another contemporaneous account can be found in Ben Macomber, *The Jewel City* (San Francisco and Tacoma: John H. Williams, 1915), 193–94. For more recent commentary on amusement areas, see the essay by Burton Benedict in *The Anthropology of World's Fairs*, 52–59; George Starr writes more specifically of the zone at the Panama-Pacific Exposition in the same volume, 154–56.

11. Edmund Wilson, 29 August 1915, quoted in Brechin, "Sailing to Byzantium," 95.

12. For a study of the classical sources of the idea of architectural character and its development in eighteenth-century theory, see chapter six, "Character," in Donald Drew Egbert, *The Beaux-Arts Tradition in French Architecture*, ed. and intro. David Van Zanten (Princeton: Princeton University Press, 1980), 121–38.

13. More on the notions of *architecture parlante* can be found in Emil Kaufmann, *Architecture in the Age of Reason* (Cambridge: Harvard University Press, 1955; repr. ed., 1968). For a concise introduction to the work

of Lequeu, see Anthony Vidler, *The Writing of the Walls: Architectural Theory in the Late Enlightenment* (Princeton: Princeton University Press, 1987), 114–24. For a more speculative approach to Lequeu, relating him to the Surrealists and especially to Marcel Duchamp, see Philippe Duboy, *Lequeu: An Architectural Enigma* (Cambridge: M.I.T. Press, 1987).

14. Nicolas Le Camus de Mézières, *The Genius of Architecture*, trans. David Britt, intro. Robin Middleton (Santa Monica: Getty Center for the History of Art and the Humanities, 1992), 70.

15. Howard Robertson, *Modern Architectural Form* (London: Architectural Press, 1932). The chapter on "Expression" is found on pp. 99–150; the quotation is from p. 134.

16. For a thorough account of Ledoux's ideal town, see "Utopia in the Countryside," in Anthony Vidler, *Claude-Nicolas Ledoux: Architecture and Social Reform at the End of the Ancien Régime* (Cambridge: M.I.T. Press, 1990), 255–361.

17. Although writings on Ledoux began to appear in Europe in the mid-1930s and an essay on him by Emil Kaufmann was published in the *Journal of the Society of Architectural Historians* in July 1943, the first major treatment of the work of both Ledoux and Lequeu to appear in this country was Kaufmann's *Three Revolutionary Architects: Boullée, Ledoux, and Lequeu* (Philadelphia: American Philosophical Society, 1952).

18. Hendrik Christian Andersen, author, and Ernest M. Hébrard, architect, *Creation of a World Centre of Communication* (Paris, 1913). Interestingly, the authors credit the phenomenon of the universal exposition – which I believe was so important to Rizzoli – as an inspiration for their ideal city.

I am grateful to Anthony Vidler for drawing this work to my attention.

19. For a lay person's posthumous diagnosis of Rizzoli as a schizophrenic, see John MacGregor, "A. G. Rizzoli, The Architecture of Hallucination," *Raw Vision* 6 (Summer 1992), 52–55.

CARDINAL: DRAFTSMAN AND SCRIBE

1. The general question of the interplay of pictorial and textual expression in Western art opens up a fertile territory which has thus far been only irregularly explored, for instance by Michel Butor in *Les Mots dans la peinture* (Geneva: Skira, 1969). Preliminary discussions of picto-scriptural production specific to Outsider Art may be found in my article "Image and Word in Schizophrenic Creation" in *Literature and the Plastic Arts 1880–1930*, ed. Ian Higgins (Edinburgh & London: Scottish Academic Press, 1973), 103–120, and in Michel Thévoz's *Détournement d'écriture* (Paris: Éditions de Minuit, 1989). I mention these sources to situate the Outsiders I have named as Rizzoli's peers: Walter Morgenthaler, M.D. *Madness and Art: The Life and Works of Adolf Wölfli* (Lincoln, Neb.: The University of Nebraska Press, 1992), 90; Jacqueline Porret-Forel, *Aloïse et le Théâtre de l'univers* (Geneva: Skira, 1993); Hans Prinzhorn, "August Klotz" in *Artistry of the Mentally Ill* (Vienna & New York: Springer-Verlag, 1972), 131–43; Lise Maurer, "Émile Josome Hodinos," *L'Art brut* 18 (1994), 152; Roger Cardinal, "Madge Gill," *L'Art brut* 9 (1973), 5–33; John MacGregor, "Henry Darger: Art by Adoption," *Raw Vision* 13 (Winter 1995/96), 26–35.

2. Apart from some rare passages of

ordinary handwriting, Rizzoli relies on capitalization throughout his texts, from the early annotated architectural designs to the verse and prose of his later years. In quoting his writings here, I felt bound to reconcile them with normal typography, though my avoidance of his resolute uppercase does create a more muted effect.

3. In a more explicit note about the *Primalglimse* composed in 1940 as part of a lengthy cycle of notes "amplifying the S series" (i.e., the cycle of early color drawings), Rizzoli refers to the sensation of his heart throbbing as if seeking to escape through his constricted throat. At the age of forty, he tells us, he was at last vouchsafed "a glimpse of the VEEAYE." We may note that Rizzoli spells the word *glimpse* correctly here, which indicates that *primalglimse* must be a magic neologism, while the private code word *veeaye* may be taken either as a shorthand for the name of the child (Virginia) or as a reference to the unsayable emblem of virginity, namely the vagina – or, of course, as both.

4. This game of substituting one word for another located at a fixed distance from it in the dictionary was played in the 1960s by a group of French literary experimentalists, styling itself as the "*Ouvroir de littérature potentielle*" ("OuLiPo" for short). The group acknowledged the influence of Raymond Roussel, arguably the most extreme case of a writer who based his work on mechanical permutations. Perhaps Rizzoli qualifies for honorary mention as an *oulipiste*!

1863
Father Innocente Rizzoli born March 14, Borgnone, Switzerland

1873
Mother Erminia (Emma) Dadami born November 11, near Valley Maggi (?), Switzerland

1885
Innocente emigrates to United States, settles in Marin County, Calif.

1889
Emma emigrates to United States, settles in Marin County

1890
Innocente and Emma marry
Son Rinaldo born

1892
Daughter Olympia born October 18

1894
Son Alfred born December 19

1895
Olympia and Alfred baptized

1896
Son Achilles (A.G.R.) born June 3

1901
Daughter Palmira born February 5, baptized

1912–15
A.G.R. moves to Oakland. Attends Polytechnic College of Engineering

1913
Olympia becomes pregnant out of wedlock. The family, except Innocente, moves to Oakland, joining Achilles

1914
Olympia marries James Codoni March 5
Olympia's daughter, Evelyn, born March 16

1915
Olympia files for divorce, citing "willful desertion"
Innocente steals gun, disappears; presumed dead; body not located
Rizzoli family moves to San Francisco; relocates seven times between 1915–33.
Panama-Pacific International Exposition opens in San Francisco

1916–23
A.G.R. joins San Francisco Architectural Club, takes classes in mechanical engineering, rendering, etc.

1919–27
Works as draftsman for Hicks Iron Works, John J. Foley and P. F. de Martini firms in San Francisco

1923
Resigns membership in SFAC

1923–33
Writes novels and short stories. Rejected by publishers, self-publishes *The Colonnade* under pen name Peter Metermaid. 3,000 copies stored and never distributed

1928–35
Does odd jobs, housework, may have been on welfare

1933
A.G.R. and Emma move to Alabama Street house

1934
Coit Tower built

CHRONOLOGY

1935
First Achilles Tectonic Exhibit opens
to the public, August
Continues as an annual exhibit in
August for next 5 years
First Symbolization drawing: *Mother
Symbolically Represented/The
Kathredal*
Work on Y.T.T.E. begins

1936
A.G.R. first view of female genitals at
age 40, April 12
Innocente's remains discovered in
Marin County, August 12, an apparent
suicide
Joins firm of Otto A. Deichmann,
architect, as draftsman
Golden Gate International Exposition
groundbreaking
Emma hospitalized for gangrenous
leg resulting from diabetes, undergoes
amputation

1937
Emma dies, January 8

1938
The Primalglimse at Forty
The Bluesea House

1939
Golden Gate International Exposi-
tion, Treasure Island
*Shirley Jean Bersie Symbolically
Sketched/Shirley's Temple*

1940
A.T.E. Portfolio, "Amplifying" the
SYMPA series
Last A.T.E. exhibit, August 4

1941
The Y.T.T.E. Home Edition

1943
The Man, The Place, The Job

1944
Final work on SYMPA series, including
Y.T.T.E.
Final work on Four Seasons series

1944–52
Works on unnamed and mostly unre-
covered illustrated prose narrative

1952
Baptized March 8
First Communion December 6

1958
AMTE's Celestial Extravag[r]anza project begins February 9, *A.C.E.* sheet 208

1961
Brother Alfred dies, leaves house to
A.G.R.

1962
Sister Palmira dies

1965
Initiates "Novella" genre

1970?
Retires from Deichmann's firm

1975
Sister Olympia dies November 30

1977
Last page of *A.C.E.* February 23,
sheet 534
Suffers stroke, is hospitalized, and
then enters nursing home in Santa
Rosa

1981
Dies November 18

Rizzoli created a number of anagrams, neologisms, and terms, many of which are listed here.

GLOSSARY

ABOHA
A Bit of Heavenly Architecture

A.C.E.
AMTE's Celestial Extravag[r]anza

Allmittizeel
Archibishop Mitty's Inheritance
Earchitecturally Expressed
Also: Almizeal

AMOTA
Architecture, Mother of the Arts

A.M.T.E.
Architecture Made to Entertain
Also: Architecture Moored to Entertain
and Architecture Manned to Entertain

Miss Amte
Personification of Architecture Made
to Entertain
Also: Marilyn Architecteur, Rechi
Tacteur, AMTE Betty Carillon, River
Archiglow, Archiglow, God's Arch
Counsel, Queen's Most Quaint,
Jesus' Prioress

Maury Architree/Architeur
Miss Amte's male counterpart

A.S.S.
Acme Sitting Station [i.e., bathroom]

A.T.E.
Achilles Tectonic Exhibit

Barbin
Female genitalia

Beamingbellabay
Birthday vision in 1961
Also: Beamingbella; later, Moffin

Bi-Pa Center
Bill-Paying Center

Bossiroam
The Cow's Precious Product

CAPS Series
Common Architecture Poetry

CARE
Comment, Analysis, Retrospection, Etc.

Carillino
Architecture

COMSAI
The Court of Many Spikes and
Intricacies (for Ben Franklin)

CONE
Comment – Origin – Notes – Etc.

CORA
Christian Order Rooting Archiglow

DAE
Daring Astronauts Elated

DAER
Decorative Architecture Entertaining
Royally

DIE
Daring Ironmen Elated [astronauts]

DOMA
Architecture

DOT
Deichmann's Oral/Orientating
Tower/Deichmann's Oriental Tour
Also: Dreaming Odes Tectonic

Dullesire
John Foster Dulles' Heavenly
Inheritance

Eagerray
Spring

Earchitecturally Expressed
Representation of a person as an architectural form
Also: symbolically sketched

EDAE
Enjoying Decorative Architecture Entertainment

Edifice del Eve
Conversion of the game of chess into an architectural edifice

Essosee
s.o.c., for Spirit of Cooperation

FOB Poetry
Free-on-Board Poetry

FOS Series
Facsimiles of Original Sketches

Gargoyle
Male genitalia

GLO
God's Lower Opal [architectural edifice for the Holy Trinity]

HOD
House of Dreams

Ibee
Information Bureau
Also: Eyebee

Il Piccolino
A.G.R.'s name for himself
Also: Little One, Littl'Un

Kathredal
Mother

Kathredal Day
Mother's Day

Kelly
California

La Fane Haspine
The Temple of Happiness
Also: the Quadrangle of Happiness

LAMA
Lost a Maternal Animation

LDL
Love's Delightful Labors

LOE
Labor's Overturer Exalting

LORA
The United States' Heavenly Inheritance: Liberty, Order, Religion – Adore

LOVE
Love of Virginity – Elating

MA
Miss Amte
Also: Mother of the Arts [i.e., architecture]

MAE
Moon Age Era

MAMA
Marble and Miss Amte [use of marble for shrines]

MANNAM
Monumental Animation Nationally Earchitecturally Expressed

MARTE
Monumental Architecture Reared to Edify

The Matriarch
Rizzoli's mother

Mazelin
Heaven [as used by the Virgin Mary]
Later: City of Kathredals

Mother of the Arts
Architecture

Nevermine
Summer

OLAF
Our Little Achilles Friend

Ollimine
Reference to sister Olympia, particularly as a mother

PAL Series
Projected Animated Landmarks

PEP
Philosophy Enriching Poetry

PIA
Contraction of Piafore [from Pinafore, one of the four main categories of drawings Rizzoli produced between 1935–44]

Ponies
Amateur poets

POPS Series
Poetry's Own Premise

Roomiroll
Autumn

SAP
Society of Ancient Prudence

SAP Series
Stabilizing Animated Premises

Sarmte
Symbolic Architectural Romance Taught to Entertain
Also: sarm, sarmtello, sarmtellei

Sayanpeau
Wait a moment

SIP
Simplifying Imagery Processing

SOA
Spirit of America

SODA
Shrine of Otto Deichmann, Architect

SYMPA
Acronym for the four categories of
drawings: Symbolizations, Y.T.T.E.,
Miscellaneous, Piafores, and respec-
tive Amplifications

TABOHA
Truly a Bit of Heavenly Architecture

TABOSA
Truly a Bit of Static Architecture

TOD
Temple of Dreams
Also: Theory/Theme of Dreams

Tokenquay
Rizzoli's architectural incarnation in
the hereafter
Also: Trokenquay

Tootlewoo
Winter

VASP
Virginity – A Shrine Potential

Veeaye
Reference to Virginia Ann (Entwistle)
Also: vagina

VOW
Virginity's Odd Wonders

Wheelingmomybay
A factory derived from the belling-
bellabay
Also: wheelingmoodybay

Y.T.T.E.
Yield to Total Elation [Rizzoli's sym-
bolic exposition]
Also: ETTY, BETTY, and TYTTE

Rizzoli employed more than three dozen different self-referential titles throughout the A.C.E., which he utilized in signing his name to almost every section of every page. Those most frequently used are listed below.

Abettor, Agent, Admirer, Arbiter, Arbitrator, Assignee, Assisting, Backer, Barker, Bearer, Beggar, Chronicler, Collaborator, Compromiser, Conformist, Contender, Conveyor, Coordinator, Corporeal Liaison, Courier, Crusader, Curator, Custodian, Customer, Decorator, Delineator, Dispenser, Donor, Draftsman, Edifier, Elevated, Embalmer, Engraver, Etcher, Fabricator, Glazier, Hack, Harpist, Harvester, Idler, Idolator, Illustrator, Incentive, Interpreter, Jelly Maker, Jogger, Journeyman, Juggler, Kapellmeister, Kettledrumer [sic], Kibitzer, Kingfisher, Lamenter, Lamppost, Lawyer, Leveller, Liaison, Limner, Luciter, Magnifier, Manipulator, Memorizer, Messenger, Musician, Narrator, Neophyte, Observer, Officiating, Organist, Organizer, Pacifier, Paraphraser, Parishioner Achilles, Patron, Peacemaker, Pianist, Poetaster, Projectionist, Promoter, Provider, Quarrier, Questioner, Quizzer, Racanteur, Raconteur, Rescuer, Retriever, Rhymster, Romancer, Scribbler, Scrivener, Sketcher, Student, Suppliant, Sympathizer, Transcriber, Translator, Trumpeter, Underwriter, Utilizer, Vendor, Violinist, Wager, Wagering, Wanderer, Whistler, Witnesser, Yodeller, Zanny, Zealot, Zephyring, Zitherist.

The following works are identified by a key that Rizzoli developed as a reference to works in his SYMPA series. Most of these applied to drawings made between 1935–44. Rizzoli subsequently listed them in the A.T.E. Portfolio and used them as a key for readers to visualize his A.T.E. installation.

In brief, S=Symbolization renderings; Y=Y.T.T.E. series; M=Miscellaneous lists, signs, and poems; P=Pia drawings, including buildings and monuments in the Y.T.T.E. series as well as portraits; A=Amplification of the fore-mentioned categories as rendered in the Achilles Tectonic Exhibit Portfolio; X=works not otherwise keyed by the artist.

S-1 *Mother Symbolically Represented/The Kathredal*. 1935. Ink on rag paper, 33¾ x 21⅞" (85.7 x 55.6 cm). Collection the estate of the artist

S-2 *Virginia Tamke Symbolically Represented/"The Tower of the Hour."* 1935. Ink on rag paper, 33⅝ x 11¾" (85.4 x 29.9 cm). Collection Helene and David Mintz

S-3 *The Spirit of Cooperation/Academically The Essosee*. 1935. Ink on rag paper, 17 9/16 x 23⅝" (44.6 x 60 cm). Collection The Ames Gallery, Berkeley

S-4 *Mrs. Geo. Powleson Symbolically Portrayed/The Mother Tower of Jewels*. 1935. Ink on rag paper, 37 x 25⅛" (94 x 63.8 cm). Collection Paul Grauberger, Belmont, California

S-5 *Irwin Peter Sicotte, Jr., Symbolically Delineated/The "Sayanpeau."* 1936. Ink on rag paper, 35⅜ x 23½" (89.9 x 59.7 cm). Collection The Ames Gallery, Berkeley

S-6 *Mother Symbolically Represented/The Kathredal*. 1936. Ink on rag paper, 27¾ x 47⅝" (70.5 x 121 cm). Collection The Ames Gallery, Berkeley

S-7 *The Mailomile/The U.S. Postal Dept., The Position of Mail Carrier in Particular, in terms of Architecture Depicted*. 1936. Ink on rag paper, 11⅝ x 35⅜" (29.5 x 89.9 cm). Collection The Ames Gallery, Berkeley

S-8 *Janet M. Peck Painted Pictorially/La Regina Della Vista Dolores*. 1937. Ink on rag paper, 26 x 39½" (66 x 100.3 cm). Collection the estate of the artist

S-9 *Mr. and Mrs. Harold Healy Symbolically Sketched/First Prize, First Anniversary*. 1936. Ink on rag paper, 35½ x 24⅝" (90.2 x 62.6 cm). Collection The Ames Gallery, Berkeley

S-10 *Alfredo Capobianco and Family Symbolically Sketched/Palazzo del Capobianco*. 1937. Ink on rag paper, 24 9/16 x 38 5/16" (62.4 x 97.3 cm). Collection The Ames Gallery, Berkeley

S-11 *Mother Symbolically Recaptured/The Kathredal*. 1937. Ink on rag paper, 30⅛ x 50¼" (76.5 x 127.6 cm). Collection The Ames Gallery, Berkeley

S-12 *Grace M. Popich Symbolically Sketched/"Little Milady Leadda."* 1938. Ink on rag paper, 25 x 35⅜" (63.5 x 89.9 cm). Collection The Ames Gallery, Berkeley

S-13 *The Primalglimse at Forty*. 1938. Ink on rag paper, 54 x 26⅝" (137.2 x 67.6 cm). Collection The Ames Gallery, Berkeley

S-14 *Mother in Metamorphosis Idolized/The Kathredal*. 1938. Ink on rag paper, 30⅛ x 50¼" (76.5 x 127.6 cm). Collection The Ames Gallery, Berkeley

S-15 *Mr. O. A. Deichmann's Mother Symbolically Sketched/Toure D'Longevity*. 1938. Ink on rag paper, 59 x 29" (149.9 x 73.7 cm). Collection The Ames Gallery, Berkeley

S-16 *Shirley Jean Bersie Symbolically Sketched/Shirley's Temple.* 1939. Ink on rag paper, 37¾ x 23⅞" (95.9 x 60.7 cm). Collection The Ames Gallery, Berkeley

S-17 *Margaret E. Griffin Symbolically Sketched/Palazzo Pianissimo.* 1938–39. Ink on rag paper, 24 x 35¾" (61 x 90.8 cm). Collection Paul Grauberger, Belmont, California

S-18 *Mother into Stone Proemshayed/ The Kathredal.* 1939. Ink on rag paper, 58¼ x 34¼" (148 x 87 cm). Collection The Ames Gallery, Berkeley

S-19 *Abraham N. Zachariah Symbolically Sketched/Sanctuary del Uncle Abe.* 1939. Ink on rag paper, 25⅝ x 35¾" (65.1 x 90.8 cm). Collection The Ames Gallery, Berkeley

S-22 *Gerry George Gould Holt/The "CADEVTR."* 1940. Ink on rag paper, 36 x 25¾" (91.4 x 65.4 cm). Collection The Ames Gallery, Berkeley

S-25 *Brother Lou and Sister Palmira Lievre Symbolically Sketched/ Palais Pallou.* 1941. Ink on rag paper, 25¾ x 35¾" (65.4 x 90.8 cm). Collection The Ames Gallery, Berkeley

Y-5 *The Y.T.T.E. Plot Plan – Third Preliminary Study.* 1937. Ink on rag paper, 37¾ x 20" (95.9 x 50.8 cm). Collection Kenneth W. K. Leung, New York

Y-8 *The Y.T.T.E. Plot Plan – Fourth Preliminary Study.* 1938. Ink on rag paper, 38¼ x 24¼" (97.2 x 61.6 cm). Collection The Ames Gallery, Berkeley

Y-9 *The Y.T.T.E. Plot Plan – Fifth Preliminary Study.* 1939. Ink on rag paper, 46 x 27¾" (116.8 x 70.5 cm). Collection The Ames Gallery, Berkeley

Y-16 *The Y.T.T.E. Home Edition.* 1941. Blueprint on paper, 4¼ x 6⅛" (10.8 x 15.6 cm). Collection Gerry George Gould Holt and The Ames Gallery, Berkeley

Y-17 *The Y.T.T.E. TABOSA Edition.* n.d. Blueprint on paper, 7½ x 11" (19.1 x 27.9 cm). Collection Shirley Bersie Lobanoff and The Ames Gallery, Berkeley

M-2 *City Hall.* 1915. Ink on rag paper, 17½ x 23¹¹⁄₁₆" (44.5 x 60.2 cm). Collection The Ames Gallery, Berkeley

M-2A *City Hall.* 1915. Ink on rag paper, 17⁵⁄₁₆ x 24⁹⁄₁₆" (44 x 62.4 cm). Collection The Ames Gallery, Berkeley

M-7 *Painted by the Sun.* 1939. Ink on rag paper, 30 x 18" (76.2 x 45.7 cm). Collection The Ames Gallery, Berkeley

M-8 *A.T.E. Colleague 1935/Accepted Emblem Design.* 1939. Ink on rag paper, 7 x 8" (17.8 x 20.3 cm). Collection The Ames Gallery, Berkeley

M-12 *Sonnet Jesus Added.* 1940. Ink on rag paper, 36 x 22¼" (91.4 x 56.5 cm). Collection The Ames Gallery, Berkeley

M-13 *A.T.E. Contents.* 1935–43. Ink on rag paper, 19 x 14¹¹⁄₁₆" (48.3 x 37.3 cm). Collection The Ames Gallery, Berkeley

M-14 *Mother Angels Proemshaying.* 1941. Ink on rag paper, 38 x 24" (96.5 x 61 cm). Collection The Ames Gallery, Berkeley

P-2 *Y.T.T.E. The Exposition Of Superior Beauty and Permanency.* 1935. Ink on rag paper, 7³⁄₁₆ x 9¼" (18.3 x 23.5 cm). Collection The Ames Gallery, Berkeley

P-13 *The Ornament.* 1936. Ink on rag paper, 17⅞ x 8⅞" (45.4 x 22.6 cm). Private collection

P-21 *The Y.T.T.E. Plot Plan – Fourth Preliminary Study Key to Plan.* 1938. Ink on rag paper, 24 x 13" (61 x 33 cm). Collection The Ames Gallery, Berkeley

P-22 *Walls del Verse.* 1937. Ink on rag paper, 19¾ x 12" (50.2 x 30.5 cm). Collection Kenneth W. K. Leung, New York

P-23 *The Bluesea House.* 1938. Ink on rag paper, 20⅜ x 30⅜" (51.8 x 77.2 cm). Collection Michael Grossman, New York

P-24 *The Eagerray.* 1939. Ink on rag paper, 5 x 8" (12.7 x 20.3 cm). Private collection, New York

P-25 *"Bridal Bar."* 1939. Ink on rag paper, 8 x 10" (20.3 x 25.4 cm). Collection The Ames Gallery, Berkeley

P-26 *The Shaft of Ascension.* 1939. Ink on rag paper, 21¹⁄₁₆ x 13" (53.5 x

33 cm). Collection The Ames Gallery, Berkeley

P-27 *Y.T.T.E. Accepted Emblem Design and Colors.* 1939. Ink on rag paper, 7 x 8⅞" (17.8 x 22.6 cm). Collection The Ames Gallery, Berkeley

P-28 *Temple of Life.* 1940. Ink on rag paper, 8⅜₆ x 5⅜" (21.1 x 13.7 cm). Collection Dr. Siri von Reis, New York

P-29 *Y.T.T.E. Information Bureau/The Ibee.* 1940. Ink on rag paper, 5⅛ x 8" (13 x 20.3 cm). Collection The Ames Gallery, Berkeley

P-31 *The Roomiroll.* 1940–43. Ink on rag paper, 7 x 8" (17.8 x 20.3 cm). Private collection, New York

P-36 *The Man.* 1943. Ink on rag paper, 9 x 6⅛" (22.9 x 15.6 cm). Collection The Ames Gallery, Berkeley

P-37 *The Job.* 1943. Ink on rag paper, 11 x 6⅟₆" (27.9 x 15.4 cm). Collection The Ames Gallery, Berkeley

P-38 *The Place.* 1943. Ink on rag paper, 10 x 6" (25.4 x 15.2 cm). Collection The Ames Gallery, Berkeley

P-39 *Mabel Bellarosa.* 1943. Ink on rag paper, 8 x 5⅞" (20.3 x 14.9 cm). Collection Didi and David Barrett, New York

P-40 *Carl P. Carppittan.* 1943. Ink on rag paper, 8⅟₆ x 5" (20.5 x 12.7 cm). Collection The Ames Gallery, Berkeley

P-41 *The Tootlewoo.* 1944. Ink on rag paper, 8 x 8" (20.3 x 20.3 cm). Private collection, New York

P-42 *The Nevermine.* 1944. Ink on rag paper, 5 x 15" (12.7 x 38.1 cm). Private collection, New York

P-43 *Virginia Gingerbred.* 1943. Ink on rag paper, 5½ x 4½" (14 x 11.4 cm). Collection Dr. Siri von Reis, New York

X-2 *Achilles Tectonic Studio.* 1935. Ink on rag paper, 8⅛ x 10½" (20.7 x 26.7 cm). Collection The Ames Gallery, Berkeley

X-3 *Virginia Ann Entwistle Symbolically Sketched/Virginia's Heavenly Castle.* 1944. Blueprint on paper, 36 x 24" (91.4 x 61 cm). Collection Virginia Bagatelos and The Ames Gallery, Berkeley

X-5 *A.T.E.* c. 1935. Ink on paper, 18 x 24" (45.7 x 61 cm). Collection The Ames Gallery, Berkeley

X-7 *Deo-Cpt-Max-Et-Dive-Marie-Virgini-Gloriose-Dei-Pare.* 1912. Graphite and ink wash on paper, 11 x 16¹⁵₆" (27.9 x 43 cm). Collection the estate of the artist

A *A.T.E. Portfolio* (Cover and 17 pages). 1940. Diazo print on paper, 34 x 18"/18 x 34" (86.4 x 45.7/45.7 x 86.4 cm). Collection The Ames Gallery, Berkeley

ACE *AMTE's Celestial Extravaganza* (Pages 208–534). 1958–77. Graphite on vellum, 24 x 36" (61 x 91.4 cm). Collection The Ames Gallery, Berkeley